GOODNEWS
from the
DUGOUT

GOODNEWS
from the
DUGOUT

TRADING A DIAMOND FOR A CROWN

Frank Minton

Illustrated by Berth-el Young

Ordering Information:

For orders and inquiries, please contact:
1-888-404-1388
www.goldtouchpress.com
book.orders@goldtouchpress.com

Printed in the United States of America

CONTENTS

Special Thanks...vii
Author's Notes..ix
About The Illustrator xii
Foreword...xiv

Chapter 1:   Step Up To The Plate.......................................1
Chapter 2:   Fans And Spectators 16
Chapter 3:   Kid's Stuff 37
Chapter 4:   Sign Him Up! 55
Chapter 5:   The Dugout Gospel...69
Chapter 6:   A Time For Every Season.................................91
Chapter 7:   At The Bottom Of The Totem Pole 99
Chapter 8:   Swing And Go For Broke!............................... 119
Chapter 9:   Baseball at its Best 132
Chapter 10: Give yourself up..144
Chapter 11: That's The Way The Ball Bounces 155
Chapter 12: In Perfect Harmony...166
Chapter 13: It ain't nothin' till I say so! 182
Chapter 14: Don't Die On Third 195

SPECIAL THANKS

D R. JOHN AND Uldine Bisagno, lifetime friends, who have walked many a mile with Joyce and me.

Dr. Morris and Jodi Chapman for their encouragement as friends, throughout life.

Jerry Craft for his personable conversation about baseball and life as we discussed his book, *Our White Boy.* He encouraged me to write more of my personal experiences.

Charles Russell, High School classmate, who shared baseball anecdotes with me.

Dan Liberthson, PhD., author of, *The Pitch is on the Way, Poems about Baseball and Life.* You may contact Dr. Liberthson, P.O. Box 31581, San Francisco, CA 94131-0581. To contact or purchase his book *liberthson@comcast.net*. A special thanks for permitting me to include five of his fine baseball poems. His words about the minor leagues inspired me to add more of my personal experiences.

Carl Erskine, great former Dodger pitcher's book, *Tales from the Dodger Dugout,* was an invaluable resource. To contact or purchase his book c.erskine17@comcast.net We recently shared spring training memories.

Hugh Poland, author of, *Steal Away,* for his many words of encouragement.

Rich Ellis, former Associate Pastor, First Baptist Church, Bellaire, Texas, for editing and solving various computer programming problems.

Beth Ludema, Author Assistant, Crossbooks, Bloomington, Indiana, for all her help and expertise.

Jerry and Dorothy Greider for years of friendship and encouragement.

Phil and Pat Scharnhorst "Hill Country" oasis friends for always being there.

Christians Jones for "tons" of work in editing and encouragement. He is editorial manager at GoldTouch press.

John and Kathy Slaymaker for help and encouragement during completion of this book.

The dugout is in fact a serious place of baseball where players spend a lot of time studying the game's opposing team. A place where teammates share knowledge with one another. The first known use of the term dugout was in 1819.

Occasionally in the dugout our conversations would turn to God and religion. Probably more so because the guys knew of my personal belief and church attendance even on the road.

Some words were given jokenly and others more sincerely. For the most part their Questions and jibes were ok. If things got a little testy I'd say "sure, I'm a church guy and saved but I'm not mad about it." Then we would all smile and go on Concentrating on the game from the dugout.

AUTHOR'S NOTES

WITH NEW BOOKS about baseball coming out every year and a few that bring in Bible material, what has a pastor with a minor league baseball career have to write about that would be of interest to a reader? Perhaps not much but out of my love for both baseball and the Bible, I had to share. Like Jeremiah of old, "Then I said, I will not make mention of Him again, nor speak any more in his name, but His word was in my heart and I could not keep silent."

This is my second book about baseball and the Bible. The first was, *Baseball's Sermon on the Mound,* I have researched and delved deeper in this effort, than in my first publication. At times, when writing this volume, I have had moments of real joy and clouds of dismay. Overall it's been a blessing to reach back and remember. I have sprinkled prose and poems among the pages that give a breath of fresh thought and insight. The Illustrations drawn by Berth-el Young have enhanced the effort with visual interest.

Throughout the book, I mention my identical twin brother, Fred. We were inseparable, until Fred was traded to the Baltimore Orioles Baseball organization. So, much of my life and baseball experiences could have been written, "We" instead of "I."

My Mother tells when Fred and I were about a year old. Up to that time we had never been separated from each other. One day mother's sister aunt Violet, decided to help mom by taking one twin to her near by home for a few hours.

Well, it didn't work as planned. The moment she drove off, her twin began to cry and wouldn't stop. The twin with mom did the same thing. In about ten minutes our aunt came back with her crying twin. Mother said, the moment aunt Violet drove up and opened the door both twins stopped crying immediately!

My twin Fred and me in our first year in professional baseball with
the Brooklyn Dodger Organization

My twin, who has a doctorate in psychology, has shared several of his poems and a few thoughts of his liking such as, "There are three universal languages; Love, Music and Baseball!" This prose of Fred's, expresses my feelings also.

I Played Baseball Once

I played baseball once
Yes, once upon a time
When it overpowered my imagination
- I was young.
One leaves the glove, the ball and
even the old "Lousville Slugger."
Walking away never wondering about the
"Take me out to the ball game" crowd
or even the seventh inning stretch.
the echo of the "Star Spangled Banner"
and the yell from the home umpire
"Play Ball," came back to me.
I searched for my baseball glove
the one that caught so many balls. I
looked for my cap with the familiar "B"
on the crown, that fit so snugly on my head
but to no avail, they were gone.
I played baseball once. Yes, once upon a
time, when it overpowered my imagination
- I was young.
Fred D. Minton, Ph.D.

During years of trials and victories, from the pitcher's mound to the pastor's pulpit, my wife Joyce, has stood with me as the Scripture says, "A help meet." From the day I met her at Wichita, Kansas North High School, I've always said, "Dear Lord, do you see what I see?" The love she has brought to the family has been a complete joy.

One might ask, "Why is Jesus so important to you?" Without hesitation I can say, "Jesus saved my soul; His Church saved my life." Even though there was a wrenching in my heart when I left the pitcher's mound, the thrill of the pastor's pulpit overshadowed that tug of war within. It was like trading a Diamond for a Crown!

As the apostle Paul said, "Now there is in store for me the crown of righteousness, which the Lord, the righteous Judge, will award to me on that day--and not only to me, but also to all who have longed for his appearing". Me too Paul!

Sometimes I wanted to restrain the call from God and play baseball another season or two. I found myself to be like the poet Robert Frost when he *penned:*

> *The* woods are lovely, dark, and deep.
> But I have promises to keep,
> And miles to go before I sleep,
> And miles to go before I sleep.
> **Robert Frost**

In December

> Our ballfield is barren now,
> Except for snow,
> Except for seeds of memories
> Of all of us who played here,
> **Gene Fehler**

ABOUT THE ILLUSTRATOR

BERTH-EL R. YOUNG IS active in the Art League and a registered professional artist. She is committed to Christ and has written and illustrated Bible lessons for many years. She feels "the sweetest part of my life is serving the Lord." Berth-el's favorite art is oil, painting realistic character portraits that tell a story. She may be contacted at youngtandb@att.net

FOREWORD

SERMON ON THE MOUND
By Leslie McLain
Southwest News, Bellaire, Texas August 8, 2000

FEW ELEVEN-YEAR OLD boys feel they have a life calling, or if they do, it usually falls between the lines of watching hometown baseball games and dime store science fiction novels. But for a young Frank Minton, who grew up in a poor neighborhood of Wichita, Kansas plagued by domestic abuse, instability, and a rapidly depleting family life, the future was clearly cut.

"God called me to preach when I was 11 years old. Never could get that out of my heart" says Minton, a graying church pastor with an instantly disarming smile spread across his face. "Sometimes I loved it and sometimes I was discouraged by it, but it was always there."

But Destiny's walk wasn't exactly a straight line to the pulpit; it made a quick stop in the minor leagues of "America's favorite past-time." Minton grew up not only with the Lord but also with the game. He and his identical twin brother, Fred, were both ball players and took their high school team to the Kansas State Championship. Both were offered athletic scholarships across the country when it came time for higher education, and both chose the University of Oklahoma.

The Minton brothers were offered Dodger baseball contracts after their college days and signed them in September 1954 with class B Ashville, North Carolina. "The year that I signed, the Dodgers were looking for a left-handed pitcher and they put out a dragnet across the country." said Minton. "When I came to spring training, among the many was one special left-handed pitcher, Sandy Koufax, who became the greatest left-handed-pitcher. So my only claim to fame was that I signed the same year as Sandy Koufax."

"My twin brother, our dad and I and the Dodger scout, Bert Wells were sitting at the little kitchen table in our house filling out the contracts. As we were talking and going over an attached questioner, it read, 'Are you willing to make baseball your life's career?' Dad, who was looking over and trying to guide everything said, 'Write down yes' and went on talking to the scout. I wrote, yes but then on the margin I wrote, 'but I will preach if God calls me'."

Minton laughs and shakes his head at the boldness of his younger self. "I knew, even then, that it was rather doubtful that baseball was going to be my life situation." Frank had signed the contract that every college pitcher dreams of, but he hadn't signed away his soul. He remained faithful to the ministry, knowing that baseball was not where he could answer the calling he felt.

But baseball was his reality, at least for then, and Minton, started pitching for the Dodger's minor league team, intent on loving every minute of it. He played from 1955 through 1957; during that time graduating from OU and getting married in that span of time. Even though the intent was to pitch in the Majors something was still missing.

"Every time I pitched I would see the crowds and be concerned about telling them about Jesus Christ. I would talk to the kids in the stands, talk to them about the Lord, and ask them where they went to church, to the consternation of some of my managers, who were very uncomfortable with that. So after three years in the minors it was easier to hear the call of God to preach."

"After three years playing the game I loved, I knew it was time to move on. So when the 1958 contract was sent to me I was reluctant to sign it. After talking to my wife and praying about it, I became a 'hold –out,' not for more money, but I had crossed a bridge; I could not go back. I turned down the contract offer. God's call had become urgent!"

"I could have still served the Lord as a baseball player, but for me it was to pastor a church and continue my education at a seminary. I was at the cross road; it was heart wrenching, sort of like trading a diamond for a crown."

"When I left baseball we built a house in Wichita, Kansas and started a Baptist church with 17 people; so at 23 I was pastor of a congregation meeting in our own house. It was wonderful!" Once again Minton cut his own words with a huge smile, going out to conquer the world with only that smile and his love of God.

Minton's transition from professional Dodger pitcher to a minister seemed simple, unadorned and he tells it with a satisfaction that can only be genuine and a distinct lack of regret. He remembers winding up every spring, feeling the tingling sensation in his arm that brought back a quick stab of longing for the mound beneath his feet, but he was never fooled. Frank Minton knew he was where his God wanted him to be.

Nine churches all over the United States were graced with the presence of a fresh, young preacher with quiet kindness and a big heart: Minton jokingly calls himself "America's pastor." He went on to say, "To be happy is one thing, but pastoring a church is a joy, which just goes beyond happiness."

Around the ministry he has made, Minton is still a star, as is clearly apparent in the affectionate tone members of his congregation take when they talk about him. Though he has lived the dream he felt God had for him, Minton remains a humbled man.

"I was not a superstar like Sandy Koufax. I knew that! But it didn't keep me from pitching. I was never a Billy Graham either, but that never kept me from preaching," he said seriously. "Every time I went out to pitch, I went out to win. Every time I go to the pulpit, I go out to win." Minton preaches a sermon twice a year in which he uses baseball to incite his congregation's interest in the gospel.

Now, pastor Minton sits confidently behind his large oak desk in an office brimming with baseball paraphernalia of all sizes and shapes. The little boy, who believed so strongly in God' plan for him, has grown up to embody it, and the joy with which he regards his life and work is unmistakable proof.

Oh Happy Day

Oh Happy Day
When Jesus Washed my sins away!
He taught me how to watch and pray
and live rejoicing every day:
Happy day, happy day
When Jesus washed my sins away!
Phillip Doddridge 1755

Illustration:
Berth'el Young's grandson with Dave Blake Young

CHAPTER 1

STEP UP TO THE PLATE

Take me out to the ball game,
Take me out with the crowd,
Buy me some peanuts and cracker jack,
I don't care if I never get back,
Let me root, root, root for the home team,
If they don't win it's a shame,
For it's one, two, three strikes you're out,
At the old ball game.

DR. JACK GRAHAM, former shortstop for Hardin Simmons University, is pastor of Prestonwood Baptist Church in Plano, Texas. He told his congregation how proud he was of his grandson, Ian, who attends a Christian preschool. "The teacher of a group of three year olds asked if someone would like to sing a song. A little girl sang the first verse of 'Jesus Loves Me.' A second little girl sang one line of the chorus, 'This Little Light of Mine.' Finally, the teacher asked, 'Is there a boy who would like to sing?' Immediately, Ian burst out singing the entire song 'Take Me Out to the Ball Game'!"

This is baseball's greatest hit. It's also baseball's national anthem. Baseball is celebrated with the singing of its rhythmic message in almost every ball park where the game is played, from Little League to the Majors. All baseball fans are familiar with it, but not everyone knows its origin.

In 1908, vaudeville entertainer Jack Norworth was riding an elevated train in Manhattan, New York when he saw a billboard that read: "Baseball today–Polo grounds." It struck him that baseball might be a good idea for an act, so he immediately grabbed a pen and paper and began scribbling the now- famous lyrics, completing them while on his short, thirty minute trip. Later, his friend, Albert Von Tilzer, set the words to music. Little did Norworth know that those hurried words would become baseball history!

Perhaps the most incredible aspect of the story is that neither Norworth nor Von Tilzer had ever seen a baseball game when they penned what would become the classic baseball song. In fact, Norworworth didn't see his first game until thirty-two years later, in 1940! With this in mind, it's amazing how Norworth was able to capture the feel of the game so completely.

To me, this heart-felt song always brings feelings of good times, shared with close friends, on laid-back summer days. This unforgettable little ditty has run through my mind hundreds of times through the years and it still makes me break out whistling! Adults and children, alike, seem to love the lyrics and tune. It's one of the songs I have personally taught my four children, usually while traveling in our car.

This trademark seventh-inning sing-along has become such a part of American history and pop culture, that the United States Postal Service commemorated this song's one hundredth anniversary in 2008 with a forty- two cent stamp.

Just as "Take Me Out to the Ball Game" has captivated America's baseball fans, in like manner, the song "Amazing Grace" has captured the hearts of Christians around the world. About the time I taught my children the baseball song, I also taught them this great inspiring Christian hymn, and both songs have become dear to their hearts.

John Newton wrote this powerful hymn in the late eighteenth century. His tombstone engraving, penned by Newton himself, is revealing: "John Newton, clerk, once an infidel and libertine, a servant of slavers in Africa … pardoned and appointed to preach the faith." This great gospel hymn sung in many churches is Newton's personal testimony.

Amazing Grace

Amazing grace! How sweet the sound
That saved a wretch like me!
I once was lost but now am found,
Was blind, but now I see.
Through many dangers, toils and snares
I have already come;
'Tis grace hath brought me safe thus far,
and grace will lead me home.
When we've been there ten thousand years
Bright shining as the sun,
We've no less days to sing God's praise
Than when we'd first begun.

As I reflect, these songs bring back two of my finest memories: *baseball and Jesus!* After all, Christianity is a singing religion. I was ten years old when I found baseball, and a year later, Jesus found me!

In 1891, Chicago White Stockings baseballer Billy Sunday said, "I would go into saloons and tank up, but Jesus Christ touched my life when I was on the streets walking past the Chicago Rescue Mission. The singing inside that old mission station stirred my heart." At twenty-seven, even though he was one of the fastest outfielders in baseball, he quit the "base path" and headed for the "sawdust trail." A few years later, he became America's best-known evangelist. The popular song "Chicago" sung by Frank Sinatra in the 1960's, gives a tip of the hat to Sunday in the lyric line "the town that even Billy Sunday couldn't shut down."

When I was four years old, war became a reality to me and remained in my life for the next seven years as World War II had just begun. Our Family was living with my dad's parents in a white two-story house on north market street in Wichita, Kansas in 1938.

My identical twin Fred and I were playing in the backyard when suddenly we heard a newsboy yelling out, "Extra! Extra! Read all about it! Nazi Germany invades Yugoslavia!"

We scampered into the house asking grandma, what was going on? Grandma was a church going believer and gave us these wondeful words of Jesus "you will hear of wars and rumors of wars but see to it that you are not alarmed." With this assurance we went back to play but War expansion continued to be a troubling part of my life with fear about the Nazi's and Hitler.

As World War II progressed, we twins made a scrapbook from pictures in the newspaper of soldiers killed in the war. Then came shock! One picture was of my 18-year-old uncle Harold Weber killed by machine-gun fire in the Anzio beachhead battle in Italy.

Embedded in my mind, on his last day of furlough dressed in his army uniform, saying a sad goodbye, "this is the last time you will ever see me," as he waved to my mom; she stood in the doorway crying.

Sunday evening December 7, 1941, at the age of seven a second war shock! Japanese airplanes had dropped bombs on the US naval base in Hawaii. The radio broadcast brought word to us from our President Franklin Roosevelt himself, "a day which will live in infamy". His unknown word "Infamy" terrified me all the more. To me, it was as if the end of the world was insight. So for years, we continued to live under the dark cloud of war.

It made me fear the Japanese peoples' nation of Japan. Ironically, I sat up late last night enjoying the opening of the 2021 Olympic games in Japan! By the grace of God, no fear of our new friends, who are baseball people par excellence. Star Los Angeles Angels Shohei Ohtani is a prime example.

Several years after the Pearl Harbor attack, our family moved to the San Diego, California area. My uncle Glen and family moved there a few months earlier for jobs were in abundance. The war scare was preparing for a possible west coast invasion. In spite of the fear, need for better economic life came first.

My uncle Glen, knowing of our economic plight, begged mom and dad to move to California. So, when he came for a quick visit with his nine year old son he urged us to go with him.

Without any preparation, all eight of us crammed into a small 1938 Chevy. Mom placed a large bedsheet, laid it on the living room and put all of our clothing, kitchen utensils, etc. She then tied the ends together and stuffed the bulging sheet into the small trunk of the car. What a miserable trip!

But the best was yet to be. We were able to move to a newly constructed government project housing right on the beach in Coronado, across the bay from downtown San Deigo. It was the best place we had ever lived!

During the war years California had become a mixed bag of people; no loyalties to make a common home place. It was like a baseball team which didn't care if they won or lost.

Small groups of boys, like street gangs, collected together. On several occasions my twin and I had to run from school "for our dear lives" to make it home.

After 15 months, sometime after the battle of the island "Iwo Jima", where the famous raising of the American Flag a top of a hill took place, we suddenly took a travel bus back to Kansas. Our family had no car. It was a sad time for me because I enjoyed living on the beach where I found "pick up" baseball. During our California beach stay I felt a better life but my dad was miserable without his cattle trading.

The Nazis surrendered in Berlin May 5, 1945; it was a joyous day! No longer fear from Hitler's terrible regime. Back to Kansas, war was still a fear for the Japanese were suicidal fighting people. Then the atomic bomb dropped on Hiroshima, Japan August 6, shook the World.

As an eleven year old boy I was almost frightened. One day before my eleventh year, August 9, 1945 a second bomb fell on Nagasaki. That was it for the Japanese nation so on the battleship USS Missouri August 15 Japan surrendered. It became known as VJ day.

As my pastor explained from the pulpit, World War II would have gone on and on with thousands of lives lost on both sides. These words did not satisfy my heart and feelings until I trusted Jesus six months later. This is where my baseball adventure was about to begin.

I learned baseball intellectually before actually playing a game. While my family and I were living in a government project in Coronado, California in 1944, toward the end of World War II, A fifth grade classmate, Tommy Flood, who knew a lot about baseball told me about a radio broadcast on KMPC. The announcer, Fred Haney, gave play-by-play accounts of the Hollywood Stars, a triple-A Pacific Coast League team.

My twin and I began listening daily. We were mesmerized as we soaked up everything about baseball. A commercial company offered a free scorebook to listeners, who would write and request one. It was a banner day when the scorebook arrived in the mail. We began scoring the ballgames faithfully.

Fred Haney was a good teacher as he took time during his broadcast to give directions on how to score. We learned most of baseball's basic symbols:

BB = base on balls	FO = force out
K = strike out	SB = stolen base
HR = home run	LOB = left on base
DP = double play	FC = fielder's choice
AC = sacrifice	E = error
RBI = run batted in	HBP = hit by pitch

We also learned the numbering system of the player positions:

1 = pitcher	2 = catcher	3 = first baseman
4 = second baseman	5 = third baseman	6 = short stop
7 = left fielder	8 = center fielder	9 = right fielder

Using the player's numbered positions, scoring could be noted as follows:

6-3 = ground out (short to first)
5-6-3 = groundout double play (third to short to first)
4-6-3 = ground out double play (second to short to first) and so forth.

Scoring those ballgames was fun and helped us learn different aspects of the game. It didn't take long to learn the names of the players and the teams in the Pacific Coast League.

Baseball is the most intellectual sports game that has been invented. The reason is, every pitch and every play changes the strategy of the game. This makes the manager's decisions extremely important and forces the players to be alert and "heads up" on every play. The game moves by strategy instead of the clock.

I got my first glimpse of professional baseball during World War II. My big day came when mom took my twin brother Fred and me to see a Pacific Coast game between the San Diego Padres and the Portland Beavers at the old wooden stadium in San Diego. We took the big ferry across the bay from Coronado to San Diego and then rode on the city bus to the park. It was a big effort for mom, but it was one of the most exciting days of my life!

I can still feel those thrilling moments of going through the turnstiles, mingling with the expectant crowds, and hearing the yells of the eager vendors, "Get your fresh roasted peanuts and Cracker Jack!" The baseball atmosphere was enchanting, and the taste of the Cracker Jack and hot dogs was unforgettable. For me, it was a day when time stood still.

Our seats were in the cheap bleachers in right field. It seemed like a mile to home plate, where most of the action was happening. At that time, I couldn't tell the difference between the second baseman and the short stop. To this day, I don't remember the score or even who won the game, but that didn't matter! It was then and there that I determined to some day wear the uniform of a professional baseball player. I was hooked!

This past June, my wife, Joyce and I went to Minute Maid Park in Houston, Texas, to take in a game between the Astros and the Pittsburg Pirates. While in the stands, it struck me, "I haven't had a bag of Cracker Jack since I was a kid in San Diego." So for $4.95 (a bit more than it cost in my younger days!), I bought a small bright red-and-white sack of memories. There it was; the same taste that sent a soft tug to my heart. It was a delight! As I crunched those Cracker Jacks I remembered my childhood America which was simpler, sweeter, easier and happier. It was a time when America, even in war, believed in "Truth, Right and God."

Jacques Barzun, a French-born American author wrote, "Whoever wants to know the heart and mind of America had better learn baseball, the rules and reality of the game." Barzun knew that baseball had so captivated the American scene in language and life that it was an intrinsic part of our culture.

Baseball movies spell out the American culture in many ways. There are six flicks that are good examples:

"The Rookie" (2002) actor Dennie Quaid a real life movie probably the fans favorite.

"The Pride of the Yankees" (1940) Gary Cooper stars as Lou Gehig whose career was cut short by the disease that bears his name.

"The natural" (1984) actor Robert Redford. A once promising Roy Hobbs a middle aged comeback cheered on by his devoted sweet heart.

"Field of Dreams" (1989) actor Kevin Costner an Iowa farmer plows up his corn field to build a baseball diamond. A voice in the movie motivated the farmer, "if you build it they will come." The idea is forgiveness for the 1919 Chicago "BlackSox" who threw the World Series to give the Cincinati Reds the series.

This movie has now a life of its own as a small baseball park seating 8,000 fans has been built in Dyersville, Iowa in a real cornfield from which the movie was made. The MLB game was played August 15, 2021 after being delayed a year by COVID19. The players from the Chicago White Sox and the New York Yankees walked out of the corn field to play a thriller with eight home runs hit during the game as the White Sox won 8 to 7.

Commissioner Rob Manfred confirmed that the Field of Dreams game will return in mid August 2022. The fan response was overwhelming, it was a hit!

"Money Ball"(2011) actor Brad Pitt. Oakland A's general manager Billy Beans figures out how to compete with home run hitters and big star players.

"42" (2019) actor Chadwick Boseman plays the real life story of Jackie Robinson's breaking the MLB color line. This movie is a favorite of mine for I was in spring Training with Jackie in 1955 and 1956 in Dodgertown, Vero Beach, Florida.

Baseball terms are used constantly in many commercial ventures. This spring in Branson, Missouri, I saw a Baptist Church marquee that read, "Put Jesus in your line up before the ninth inning."

Even families are into baseball culture. Travis and April Ficklin of Bloomington, Indiana have named their three boys after famous major league players: Rollie (Fingers) Nolan (Ryan), and Brooks (Robinson). Only an American would catch the symbolism of their names.

Even Cartoons reflect how baseball is ingrained into American culture. World fame cartoonist, Charles Schults most popular comic strip "Peanuts" put smiles on all our faces with understanding! In one cartoon Snoopy is lying on his dog house thinking, "My life has no meaning." The next few frames he continues to moan, "Everything has no meaning" He sighs "no meaning."

Suddenly Charley Brown appears with a baseball glove . Immediately Snoopy gleefully hollars out "ah! meaning!!"

On a Serious note it reminds me of the Bible quote in Ecclesiastes, "I have seen all things under the sun; all of them are meaningless". So true for those who are living in their own empty strength.

Jesus promised "I have come that you may have life and life abundantly". In other words more of life than you ever had in all of life! It means - Life does have meaning on and off the baseball diamond!

How important is baseball history anyway? How did this game earn its place in the hearts of Americans? Where did it get started and who invented it, if anyone? Was it a creation or a continuation?

Harvard professor Stephan Jay Gould, in his provocative book, *Triumph and Tragedy,* gives an anthropologist's view of the beginning of baseball. Gould writes, "Stories about beginnings come in only two basic modes. An entity has an explicit point of origin, a specific time and place of creation, or else it evolves and has no definable moment of entry into the world." After much research, Gould went on to write, "Baseball developed from a plethora of previous stick-and-ball games. It has no true Cooperstown and no Doubleday." Finally, he gives no retreat, "The beginning of baseball is a creation myth."

Walt Whitman in 1846 wrote, "Through the outer parts of Brooklyn, we have observed several parties of youngsters playing 'base,' a certain game of ball. We wish such sights were more common among us." Little did Whitman know that baseball was going to spread like a prairie wild fire across America!

George F. Will in his book, *Bunts,* writes, "President Lincoln interceded for boys who were being shooed off the White House lawn for playing baseball. The Civil War, which moved millions of young men hither and yon, acquainting them with the variety of American experiences, simultaneously spread baseball like honey across bread." There is a most intriguing account from *Uncle John's Reader,* "When Geronimo escaped from a reservation near Fort Apache, Arizona Territory in 1886, soldiers had to stop a baseball game to saddle up."

In the early 1900's America was still distancing itself from the influence of England. So, in the eyes of some, the game dubbed "America's Pastime" had to be seen as all-American from beginning to end. That's when a former baseball pitcher Albert Goodwill Spalding, who later became a sporting goods magnate, stepped up to the plate with a personal mission and hand picked a committee in 1907, to ensure that baseball would be viewed as an original American sport.

The "blue ribbon" committee was chaired by A.J. Mills and included several prominent businessmen and two senators, who had also served as presidents of the National league. Their investigation, however, was biased from the beginning, thus making much of their research untrustworthy from a historical perspective. Their conclusion in 1913 was distinguished United States General Abner Doubleday as the originator of the game in Cooperstown, New York in 1839. This was presumptive, at best. Most sports scholars have discovered that there is little, if any, evidence that this committee's findings were true.

Interestingly, Doubleday never claimed to have invented baseball, nor to have any knowledge of it, or even played the game! In fact, at the time he was supposed to have been in Cooperstown inventing the game, he was actually at West Point as a first-year Army student. Further, Doubleday left volumes of diaries and other writings that never once mentioned the game of baseball. Those who knew him say he was a studious young man who spent his time in bookstores, and whose hobby was making maps of the New York countryside. His only recorded connection with baseball came, as an Army General during the Civil War when he placed an order for baseball equipment at the request of the soldiers.

When you consider the facts, it's really a travesty of justice to credit Doubleday with baseball's origin. Donald Honig, in his book, *Baseball America,* writes with sarcasm, "Abner Doubleday didn't know a baseball from a kumquat."

The spread of baseball continued throughout the days of World War II. At that time, tradition still gave Abner Doubleday of Cooperstown, New York, the nod as being the "father of baseball." The bleacher fans believed it and as a ten year old boy, I bought it hook, line and sinker. However, baseball historians, George Vecsey, Leonard Koppett and John Thorn all agree, that according to their research, it was almost impossible for Doubleday to have created baseball. The erroneous history is still alive and fostered across the land by sports enthusiasts. My brother-inlaw, Bob Buck told me one of The Doubleday Sports Bar in the south Texas, Gulf Coast town of Port Isabell. This bar has become a popular museum with all kinds of memorabilia, from wall murals of baseball legends, down to the traditional history of Doubleday, printed on the back of the menu.

For those who insist on pinpointing a specific person as "Father of the Game," the most likely culprit is Alexander Joy Cartwright. He was a bank teller and fireman in New York, who was inducted into Baseball's Hall of Fame in 1938. According to Harvard professor Stephen Jay Gould, "His codification defined the beginning of our national sport." Cartwright changed the baseball field from a square to a diamond, laid out the ninety foot dimensions of the baseball infield, ruled three strikes for an out and nine innings for a game.

The first game played under Cartwright's rules was at the Elysian Fields in Hoboken, New Jersey on June 19, 1846. His New York Knickerbockers club of upper crust professionals took a ferry across the Hudson River to New Jersey to play against a pick-up team called the New York Nine. The Knickerbockers lost to the New York Club 23-1. This was the first and last time that baseball was played as a "gentlemen's" game! From that time on it became a game to win. Cartwright's rules standardized the game, so that even with his British heritage, the game became Americanized.

Yet, the steamrolling Spaulding and his hand picked committee made Doubleday its hero. Thus, baseball's Hall of Fame is located in Cooperstown, New York on the false premise that Doubleday played the first baseball game there.

An early baseball pioneer, Henry Chadwick, who later became editor of the *Spaulding Guide*, wrote that baseball had directly descended from a British children's stick and ball game called Rounders, a close resemblance to the British game Cricket. His reasoning was more truth than the Doubleday fiction but because he also had a British connection, his research was quickly dismissed. In the spirit of the day, America's signature sport had to be purely American and not tainted with British origin. Chadwick stood his ground and stated, "An English origin did not distract one iota from the merit of the game." Another quote from Chadwick is fascinating, "Baseball never had no 'fadder;' it jest growed." I agree wholeheartedly and for me, baseball is still the great American game, regardless of its origin.

To give credence to the English influence, there are at least two literary evidences of a forerunner game. First, Charles Carroll Hudson, mentions a catchy little poem in a book entitled, *A Little Pretty Pocket Book,* published in England in 1744, that could muddy the American waters. It appears that a children's game existed, at least resembling American baseball, nearly one-hundred years earlier when this anonymous poem was written:

> The Ball once struck off,
> Away flies the Boy
> To the next destin'd Post,
> And then Home with Joy

Second, Professor Gould, provides additional evidence for a British origin dating back to a novel written by Jane Austen in 1797. In her book, *Northanger Abbey*, Austen writes of various contests based on hitting a ball with a stick and scoring by running around bases.

Pinpointing the origin of baseball has long baffled diligent sports enthusiasts. But to the average fan, the origins of baseball mean very little, if anything. To us, the game is as exciting as ever. In fact, how little we know of the game's history doesn't make or break our enjoyment of it one iota. Fans don't care who used to play; they care about who plays *now*. Using the time honored Bud Abbott and Lou Costello's entertaining jargon (which is now enshrined at Cooperstown), it's "Who's on first" *now* and "what's on second" *now,* that really counts. Even last year's win and loss records have little impact. There's always a new season where the, "thrill of victory and the agony of defeat," bring excitement and enjoyment for fans of all ages. Every game makes its own history!

According to, *Baseball Between the Numbers,* Jonah Keri writes, "Baseball layout and rules did not just happen. It took at least a century to get everything as we have it today. Baseball has brought an ever changing world to the game, from new stadiums, players, owners, traditions, spring training camps and post season play. Together they almost make the game unrecognizable and yet its stability stands throughout the seasons of 'Play Ball'."

The US doesn't have an official sport but it does have a national pastime. It has historical significance and cultural value. It's more relaxed than other sports because it has a leisurely pace of enjoyment.

Maintaining baseball image as a wholesome American pastime, MLB is rightly cracking down on any kind of cheating. Cheating damages American faith in the game. An unfair competitive advantage gives an uneven playing field. Baseball has been a family-friendly sport so integrity and fairness continue to give family value as a key to our favorite pastime.

MLB commissioner Rob Manfred is learning fast that cheating can no longer be tolerated, Pitchers with a foreign substance on their lingerie included.

So, who cares about the Who, What, When, Where and Why of baseball's origin, as long as we enjoy the great American sport? To some, however, baseball is much more than a game, for they revere it as a religion. A San Francisco pitcher who had finally made it to the majors after years in the minors said disappointedly, "They said every thing in life would be different when I made it to the Bigs, but now that I am here I feel as if I have been ripped off." There are many life lessons you can learn from it; but in the end, baseball can only reflect and imitate. The game itself is not real life.

It's a whole different ball game when it comes to true religious faith. The five W's matter when we speak of life and eternity. Myth and speculation have no place when a person's soul is in the balance. Christianity is founded upon truth not myth and there is no intention by believers to deny the true roots of Christianity.

Since Christianity is the revealed religion, Christians gladly look back to the Old Testament prophets who had long proclaimed the coming of the Messiah, the Anointed One, the Christ. The prophets blended the near and far horizon to perfectly forecast the coming of the Messiah, the Christ and what he would do. Believers hold firmly to prophetic truths concerning Jesus.

Even without knowing about the true "Father of the Game," baseball can still be enjoyed to the fullest by any smiling kid with a ball and bat. But it is impossible to enjoy life to the fullest without a personal relationship with life's founder, who is Jesus Christ. He is the Author and Finisher of the Faith. Many world religions talk about God, but only in Jesus Christ, can a person truly *find* God.

Jesus said, "When you see me, you see the Father. No one comes to the Father but through me and I and my Father are one."

How could Jesus say these things? He could say them because even before the creation of the universe, He existed. Look at the evidence from the Bible. The book of John says, "In the beginning was the Word, and the Word was with God. He was with God in the beginning." Scripture tells us that Jesus is the Word and, therefore, the originator of both creation and Christianity.

Throughout the Bible's New Testament, the writers declare that Jesus Christ is the founder of both life and faith. For by him all things were created: things in heaven and on earth, visible and invisible all things were created by Him." Therefore, what you might call, "the game of life," has its origin in Jesus Christ. He said of himself, "I am the way, the truth, and the life. No one comes to the Father except through me."

When I officiate at a funeral, I close the service with this phrase:

> Without the way, there is no going,
> Without the truth, there is no knowing,
> Without the life, there is no living!

Baseball will always be fun to play as long as you have smiling kids with a ball and bat. They will continue to make their own history with stick and ball games whether in school yards, corner lots or city streets. That's why baseball is destined to go on and on and on!

Christianity is a forever life of enjoyment that causes happy-faced kids to skip and sing, "Jesus loves me, this I know, for the Bible tells me so." These happy, singing kids will continue to pass on the Good News at home, school and around the world. Therefore, Christianity is destined to go on and on and on until Jesus comes again!

> Jesus loves me! This I know,
> For the Bible tells me so
> Little ones to Him belong;
> They are weak, but He is strong.
> Yes, Jesus loves me,
> Yes, Jesus loves me,
> Yes, Jesus loves me,
> The Bible tells me so.
> **Anna Bartlett Warner**

CHAPTER 2

FANS AND SPECTATORS

"Then from 5,000 throats and more there rose a lusty yell;
It rumbled through the valley, it rattled in the dell;
It knocked upon the mountain and recoiled upon the flat,
For Casey, mighty Casey, was advancing to the bat."
Ernest Thayer
(Excerpt from Casey at the Bat)

THIS EPIC POEM about a beloved slugger, who had his chance to make the Mudville hometown fans happy, has become a symbol for all towns and cities that dare to have their hearts broken by the swing of a bat. But baseball would be little more than kids at play if it were not for their fans, who at times become a bit too involved in the game. Players may love 'em or hate 'em, but there wouldn't be any professional baseball, without those fans and spectators, who pay to watch the games. They are the ones who keep the turnstiles moving, the concession stands busy and most of all the money to pay the freight to run the games. An old baseball axiom is "Fans won't come if the home team doesn't win."

According to Pete Palmer and David Nemec in, *Fascinating Baseball Facts,* baseball spectators were originally called Kranks. Around 1883, St. Louis Browns manager, Ted Sullivan, coined the term, "fan" when team owner Chris Von deer Ahe referred to the Browns' rooters as fanatics. David Nemec, baseball historian and author continued, "Being a spectator at the time could be a risky business. There was no fence back of home plate to protect the fans. The stands back of the plate were known as "Slaughter Pens" because so many fans who sat there were felled by foul balls."

Fans were charged for the first time to see a baseball game when approximately 1,500 people paid ten cents each to see the New York All Stars play the Brooklyn All Stars. The game was played at the Fashion Race course in Long Island on July 20, 1869.

Fans love to get a personal autograph from their favorite ball player. When I was playing pro ball, it was always a good feeling to have kids lean over the stands and ask for my autograph. I always tried to honor their requests. In fact, under my signature, I wrote Rom 1:16. This verse says, "I am not ashamed of the Gospel of Christ for it is the power of God to all who believe."

When it came to giving out autographs there was never a more accommodating signer than Babe Ruth, especially when the autograph seekers were kids. Even when some of the fans were unruly and rude, the Babe would just laugh and sign his name. Can you imagine what those little scraps of paper would be worth today?

There is something special about the home team crowd to a ball player; it's like a welcome home banner. Even the playing field and grandstands seem warm and friendly, as if they are ready to shake your hand. When a player looks occasionally in the stands and spots a baseball jersey with his number and name, it shows him, "Hey, they like me, they really do like me!" Players actually need pats on the back to encourage them to get out on that diamond and give their best. Leo "The Lip" Durocher, one of the most competitive ball players of them all, once quipped, "I cannot play to empty benches." Fans are the main reason that a team wins more games at home than on the road.

When I was playing with the Dodgers baseball Minor League, I always joined a hometown church. When possible, I visited and worshipped in other churches. But there was something more inviting and warmer in my home church where I fellowshipped with other believers. I needed their spiritual strength to help me walk closer to Jesus.

For most of the 2020 season Covid 19 had almost emptied, the stands to 90 percent or less of the usual attendance with some fans wearing face masks and sitting at least six feet apart from each other. Families or close friends huddle together to make baseball feel more normal. In some parks the front row of seating have bigger than life cardboard faces of fans who had contributed to the teams benevolent charity funds. The teams benevolent charity funds have increased dramatically to help fight the Covid 19 during 2021.

Before the pandemic, a welcomed sight, in Houston Astros' Minute Maid Stadium were fans located in the left field crawford boxes called, "The Posse". Each wore a large brimmed Mexican straw hat. A home made banner above them spelled out horse in Spanish, "El Caballo." Several of these faithful fans carried stick horses. They were a favorite fan base for more than thirty years.

I found that pastors often need that kind of encouragement as they face their congregations each Sunday. Some years ago, Joyce and I took a vacation with grandchildren, Gloria and Alejandro, to Galveston, Texas. On Sunday morning, I went to worship at the First Baptist church. The pastor was a young man who preached with intensity. As he preached he suddenly began to sob. He was so overwhelmed with the meaning of his message, he dropped to one knee beside the pulpit and continued crying. The congregation was stunned! Silence swept across that large worship center as we sat in awe. You could have heard a pin drop!

I knew the young man needed help. But what could I do? I was only a visitor. Finally, mustering all of my courage I hollered out, "Preach on, pastor, preach on!" Suddenly, the august congregation broke out in a loud applause with cheers and even whistles! It sounded as if we were in a baseball stadium cheering a game winning hit. Those sounds from the usually quiet, formal congregation, resounded to the pulpit area. The young pastor looked up in amazement, as they continued their response. He slowly rose, stood at the pulpit and finished his sermon with enthusiasm! He needed some real fan encouragement.

> At the closing of his message the usual invitation resulted in dozens from the congregation who came forward to the altar area to make personal decisions for Christ! After the service when I picked up Joyce and the Kids I said, "Honey, I just preached the best sermon of my life in only five words, "Preach on Pastor, Preach on!"

The church event continued like an exciting extra inning baseball game! As we were standing in line to order our lunch I recognised a young couple in front of me who had attended the worship service. I commented, "say, did y'all go to church today?"

"Sure did," came the man's response and he continued, "God was there" His words not only humbled me but actually almost frightened me!

When I was a boy growing up, I never rooted for the New York Yankees. I was like jovial manger, Tommy Lasorda of the Los Angles Dodgers, "When I bleed, I bleed Dodger Blue." But to my surprise, one day in New York, I found myself rooting for all I was worth for those darn Yankees.

My grandchildren, Gloria and Alejandro, then attending New York Law School and American University in D.C., invited me to the American League Divisional playoff game on October 9, 2009, between the Yanks and the Minnesota Twins. "If you can get the tickets, I'll be there!" My granddaughter got last minute tickets three levels up in section 328.

With a packed crowd, in the new billion dollar Yankee Stadium, I watched one of the most exciting games of my life! In the seventh inning with the Twin's ahead 3-1 and runners on first and second, the Twins batter hit a shot into right field for a hit and it looked like a sure run would be scored. It would have been doom's day for the Yankees if it were not for an unusual pick off play, engineered by their star short stop, Derek Jeter. He took the relay from the outfielder and looked to throw the runner out at the plate, but instead, seeing the runner coming from first had overran second base, he immediately flipped the ball to Johnny Damon at second, who tagged the runner out, a moment before the Twins player going home could score. It was an absolute gem by a future Hall of Famer. The inning was over and that play set it up for the thriller in the Ninth.

The Yankees entered the ninth still behind 3-1. With two outs and no one on, "it looked mighty grim for the hometown nine." Then, first-year man, Mark Teixeira singled to right and up came Alex Rodriquez, like "mighty Casey at the Bat." The stadium went wild with cheering. "Knock it outta' the park!" came the cry from a fan behind me. Then, a resounding "crack" reverberated all over the stadium. A-Rod's swinging bat sent a line drive missile over the right field fence! The game was tied 3-3; new life for "Mudville!"

At that moment the celebration began! All 52,325 fans with one thunderous voice instantly chanted, "New York!" and spontaneously clapped as they drummed out, "Clap, Clap–Clap, Clap, Clap! New York!" The chant went on and on even as the game proceeded into the tenth and eleventh innings. Mark Teixeira, again came to the plate as lead off batter for the Yankees, in the bottom of the eleventh. On the first pitch, he hit a drive off the top of the left- field wall and into the rollicking sell out crowd, ending the game with a "walk-off" home run! AP News reported, "Mark Teixeira and Alex Rodriguez stood together as Yankee Stadium roared." Now the chant surged on with new lyrics, "Yankees win! Clap, Clap. . . Clap, Clap, Clap, Yankees Win!" Over and over, again and again they chanted!

The New York fans just couldn't do enough celebrating. We all stayed and stood in section 328 three levels above the playing field, for at least five minutes, as if we had won the game ourselves. As we walked out to the gates to ride the subway to Lower Manhattan, the public address system was playing Frank Sinatra's version of "New York, New York." My grandchildren and I sang right along with him. The party continued as we crammed our way into the subway on our way home.

It was a glorious New York Yankee night! I became one of them because I too had experienced a Yankee baseball night. I was so caught up with the emotion of that packed stadium that before I knew it, a Dodger guy from Texas, became one of those New York Yankee fans. I never would have believed it! Those excited, romping, stomping bunch of die hard fans caused me to be one of them. The celebration continued as Derek Jeter and Andy Petit led the Yankees to win it all, to become the 2009 World Series Champs! My grandchildren and I felt extra pride with their win. Andy Petit sings in the choir of a Baptist Church in Channelview, Texas.

The Bible tells us that being present made a big difference in the life of Thomas, one of the disciples of Jesus. All the living disciples, except for Thomas, were huddled together in fear after Jesus had risen from the grave. Since the door was locked, they were doubly surprised when Jesus appeared in the room and said, "Peace be with you!" Then He showed them his hands and his side. The disciples were overjoyed!

Later, they saw Thomas and told him, "We have seen the Lord!" But Thomas said "Unless I see the nail marks in His hands and put my finger where the nails were, and put my hand in His side, I will not believe it."

A week later, the disciples were again in the house and this time Thomas was with them. The door was locked, yet again, Jesus appeared among them and said, "Peace be with you." Looking at Thomas, He said, "Put your finger here; see my hands. Reach out your hand and put it into my side. Stop doubting and believe."

Thomas exclaimed, "My Lord and my God!" Then Jesus said, "Because you have seen me, you have believed; blessed are those who have not seen me and yet have believed." We are blessed!

Sitting in my living room and watching the Yankees play baseball on television, has its place. I must admit though, watching them play in their stadium that evening made me a long lasting fan, after the Dodgers, of course!

Christian fellowship is a God given blessing. First Montgomery Baptist Church in Texas has a drive-in worship service to cope with the COVID 19 virus. The church has built a two story platform for the pastor, Chris Gober and music director Jon Steptock with a small band. In place of the usual "amen" response, the congregation honk their car horns!

The worshippers tune their car radios to a FM station and hear the entire service. It has been so popular and a good outreach to outsiders that the church has plans to continue the drive in.

Likewise, personally attending church services for worship has the same effect. Sitting at home watching a TV worship service cannot make the same impact as being present at church. "Hey baseballers, don't miss Jesus!" Jesus said: "For where two or three are gathered together in my name, I will be there also."

You will find fans from every walk of life. Dr. Stephen Jay Gould, Harvard professor and renowned critic of theatre was a most unlikely baseball fan. Yet his terrific baseball book, *Triumph and Tragedy,* gives insights about baseball that could come only from an ardent devotee of the game. Another fan of great interest is, Sean MacBride, a Nobel Peace recipient and Irish play-write who wrote, "What's surprising and delightful is that spectators are allowed, and even expected, to join in the vocal part of the game."

There are innumerable baseball fans among those serving time in prison. In 1956, when I was pitching for the Dodger farm club, the Great Falls, Montana Electrics, I was invited by the chaplain to speak at the Idaho State Penitentiary in Boise. The prisoners usually listened to radio broadcasts of the Pioneer League games and the announcer got their attention when he mentioned, I was preparing to become a Baptist preacher. The prisoners asked the chaplain to invite me to come to their chapel service. Since I had never been in a prison situation before, I asked him, "What should I do when we meet the prisoners." He said, "Smile; no one smiles here." When I spoke to them about baseball and the Bible, they gave me rapt attention and enthusiastic applause when I finished. Baseball and the Bible brings all types of people together.

At the close of my message a prisoner asked the chaplin if he could give a testimony. It was aweome! The chaplin warned the men that whatever they said in the chapel would be out in the yard before the service was over. Immediately, just like popcorn popping , prisoner after prisoner gave personal words in the name of Jesus. I was struck with their devotion in face of certain persecution!

Getting home town fans to respond with noise and enthusiasm is promoted by every club. At the Astros Minute Maid Park in Houston, Texas, we are electronically urged to join in as the word "noise" is flashed upon huge screens. Across many major league stadiums the trumpet sound of "Charge" is heard from the speakers to rally the crowd to yell back in unison, "Charge!"

A listless crowd at a game is a yawn. I remember when my life long friend, Dr. John Bisagno and I took in a Houston Astros game, at the now retired Astrodome. The Astros were in sixth place and about twenty games out of first place. Being late August, the crowd was somewhat sparse. As we were sitting a few rows above the dugout, we leaned back and put our feet over the empty seats in front of us. In the third inning, it was so quiet, a woman asked her husband, "Honey, when is the game going to start?"

Late September

Day game, midweek,
shank of the season,
home team sinking third,
visitors headed cellar-ward
and my slow season
passing too.
Attendance sparse
(pick a seat, put up your feet),

shrill whistlers rare,
cursing zealots gone,
and even the umps'
screw-ups mildly tolerated.
Neither fans nor players
have anything to prove.
Massive calm
between time's unleashed
glaciers.

Win or lose
doesn't matter, only
warm sun
blue sky
green grass.
Ball thwacks leather,
bat cracks ball,
players circle eternal.
I could stay forever,
finally coming home.
Dan Liberthson

Spectators are fickle, even selfish. They don't want the best team to win; they want their team to win. If a team slips into the cellar, the enthusiasm turns to jeers and finally they vacate the stadium altogether. For all it's worth, Yogi Berra is reported to have said, "If people don't want to come to the ball park, nobody's going to stop them." He also said "No one goes there anymore, because it's too crowded." On the other hand, Lou "Lippy" Durocher said, "I can't play before an empty stadium." He sure would be in bad shape today with all this COVID 19 swerving around!

Jesus understood the fickleness of the crowds. The Bible says "Jesus would not entrust himself to them for he knew all men!" Even when he chose his disciples he knew which one would betray him. Yet, Jesus steadfastly set his face to go to the Cross, whether they followed him or not.

The crowd that joyfully praised God for Jesus when he entered Jerusalem and shouted "Hosanna, in the highest," was the same crowd, who later shouted, "Crucify Him!" as he stood before Pilate.

Regardless of the noise of the crowd, a player must continue to focus on the game. Boos and derision, even though hurtful, should not break his concentration. A rookie must learn not to have "rabbit ears" when he is on the playing field.

During my freshman year at the University of Oklahoma, our coach, Jack Baer wanted to test my concentration. In an intra-squad game he had the entire dugout ride me, while I was pitching. It was disheartening to hear my own buddies scorn me. As you can imagine, I struggled with composure and my pitching became shaky. It was a good lesson for me. I learned you must shut out distractions.

In a Peanuts cartoon by Charles M. Schults, Charley Brown is pitching in a baseball game and says to himself, "This is it...if we get this last out, we win...if he hits one we lose. Snoopy is playing in the outfield, a high fly ball is hit to snoopy, if he catches it, we win!! Snoopy says to himself, "no problem". Just then someone on the side lines with a big mouth hollers out, "Hey, who's the short stop with the big nose?"

Snoopy hearing the guy looks over at him just as the ball was coming down. Instead of catching the ball it hits snoopy on the nose, "Bonk!"

Old time ball player, Ty Cobb, had a mean disposition and a bad case of "rabbit ears." On occasions, he would charge the stands and actually attack heckling fans. His behavior gave baseball many a black eye. Yet in 1936 he was inducted into the baseball Hall of Fame along with Babe Ruth.

Thank the Lord for the great pitcher Christy Matherson who in the early 1900's saved baseball's image by being a perfect hero for kids. His Christian life on and off the field made him known as the "Christian gentleman ball player." A day after his death, the stadium band played the Christian hymn "It is well with my soul."

When I played teenage baseball in Kansas it was the Ban Johnson league. I was proud to play in the league when I learned Ban Johnson, who organized MLB's America League, demanded that players and fans be ejected for being rowdy. He helped make baseball become a family affair.

Completely out of character, James and John wanted Jesus to "Send fire down out of heaven to consume" some Samaritans who would not welcome them. But Jesus said, "Let them alone, if they are not against us then they are for us!" To have convictions is to be commended, but to become retaliatory in your belief, regardless how sincere you may feel, is not true Christianity. The Scripture is clear, "In your anger do not sin." On occasions, when my teammates and I would have differences of opinion about what we believed, I often would try to be conciliatory by saying, "I'm saved, but I'm not mad about it."

A child's Christian song sings

> In my heart to this very day
> I've got that joy, joy, joy, joy
> Down in my heart
> Down in my heart
> Down in my heart
> To stay!

Almost every fan has a personal baseball story he likes to tell. I am sure that most of us have our own "Field of Dreams" story. In fact, David Cantoneo's book, *Fans Oral History,* is chuck full from beginning to end with ordinary people telling their favorite baseball stories.

My younger brother, Clark, lying on his death-bed told me his favorite sports story. Since he was a three sport star in high school, I had no idea what kind of story he would tell. He asked, "Do you remember our baseball pick- up games, we played at Waco Avenue School back home? I was eight or nine years old and you guys were seven years older. Some of those bigger guys complained about me wanting to play. 'He's too little,' they claimed. But you and Fred had a rule, 'If I couldn't play, you guys wouldn't play either.' Well, together, we were one-third of a team. If I didn't play, there wouldn't be a game, so I always got to play! It meant they would usually put me in right field and bat ninth, but that was O.K. My big brothers always took good care of me." His favorite baseball story totally and pleasantly surprised me.

One of the Houston Astros' ardent fans is Earl Folgar. He wears a prosthesis on his left leg. Even with this handicap, Earl and his wife make it up to the third level of Minute Maid Park, to their season ticket seats. Earl has the Astros' star logo professionally painted on his prosthesis. Now they are real fans!

Verle Petri, Houston insurance executive, tells of the time in 1943, when he was fifteen years old, living near Des Moines, Iowa. "A buddy and I, managed to get a car and drove to St. Louis to watch an exhibition game of the Cardinals. This gave us the opportunity of seeing some of our favorite players in action, Enos Slaughter and Stan Musial in particular. Stan Musial at that time had not been declared the first baseman for the team, so he played right field.

An opposing player hit a home run high up into the left field stands. The moment the ball was hit, Enos knew it was gone, so he never moved a muscle as he watched it. Slaughter made the game look so easy, I thought, 'Hmm, baseball is for me.' So, at eighteen, I signed a pro contract with the Chicago Cubs farm team and after two years, found it wasn't all that easy!"

My favorite baseball story happened at Dodger stadium on April 25, 1976. I was not present but it's an event that has been played many times on TV and the Internet. In fact, it has been declared as one of the top 100 Major League moments.

Rick Monday, center fielder for the Chicago Cubs gave his personal account of what happened. "It was the top half of the fourth inning with two outs and one ball on the batter, when two men, a father and his teenaged son, broke through security and ran out onto the outfield carrying a kerosene soaked American flag. They both knelt down and began striking a match, attempting to burn it. Fortunately the wind blew it out. Seeing what was about to take place, I immediately raced over and snatched the flag away before they could light a second match." Monday, remembering his heroic action said, "I picked it up still on the run! I gave the flag to Doug Rau who was a left handed pitcher who had come out of the third base dugout. I turned around and saw the guys being escorted off the field by members of the security team.

It was a very quiet moment, then there came a smattering of applause, one part of the stadium stood and another and another from every part. Then kind'a collectively the people began to sing, "God Bless America!" former Dodgers Rick Monday's dash to save the flag of the United States of America, thrills my baseball American heart to this very day!

"Afterward Monday said," the only thing certain is they'll play the National Anthem before every game." If only Rick's words were a truism. Shame on the ball players who refuse to stand for our National Anthem and Flag.

Yes, as a former Dodger minor leaguer, I stood with my hand over my heart every time our National Anthem was played before our games. It is interesting to note that the Star Spangled Banner was played in ball parks all over America in 1919 before it became our National Anthem 1931. But sadly, as I view the American scene very few things are sacred anymore, even in sports!

At every major League game, fans proudly wear the jerseys of the home team with their favorite player's name and number on the back. From little babies to old codgers in their 80's they proudly wear their hero's name and number.

Teenager Hunter Leum, is center fielder for his Brownsbridge high school team. Off the field he enjoys wearing the team jersey of his favorite Los Angeles player, Torii Hunter. When asked why he wears the shirt, Leum answered, "In this way I feel I can share in his runs, hits and errors. He hits 20 or more homeruns every season and he has been a Golden Glove outfielder for ten consecutive years. He plays center field just like me, and of course. I like his name Hunter, just like my first name."

Brent Musberger, is one of my favorite national television sports announcers. I first heard him in the 1960's when he was at a station in Dallas, Texas. To my delight, I found he is more than an announcer, he is a real fan. Brent said, "I am a sports junkie; if I wasn't at the game itself, I'd be in front of a large screen television set."

A real fan is a "say so" baseball enthusiast. Win or lose, they declare their loyalty, "come what may." Likewise, the Bible says, "Let the redeemed of the Lord say so!" We need a lot of "say so" Christians. The Apostle John gives us the same message, "We proclaim to you, what we have seen and heard, so that you may also have fellowship with us."

Home town fans are proud of their team and feel they belong to it as much as any player. True fans, are well informed and love to get into conversation about their team. They like to discuss the hit-and-run, the infield fly rule, and other technicalities of the game. Fans don't simply watch the ball, they watch the fielders, the runner taking his lead, and the third base coach flashing signals. They know to cheer when a batter bounces out to first, yet advances the runner. Their booing erupts when a possible double play results in only a single out. Fans feel they know the right game strategy and are not afraid to let their feelings be known. In fact, some of the most knowledgeable fans are those sitting in the farthest corner of the stadium, carefully focusing on all that is going on and registering each play on their 1 phone.

There are times, that try a fan's soul. Even real fans may blow their top at their beloved team, when it goes into a slump and loses ten or more in a row. Yet, these same irate fans do finally forget and forgive. It is difficult to love a losing baseball team, but real fans never give up. Their attitude is like the Salvation Army's slogan, "A man may be down, but he is never out!"

Baseball Fan's Lament

Things are really looking black –
Home team's getting off the track.
Everything is out of whack –
Paying players all that jack.
Jean H. Berkompas

The crowds that followed Jesus were like spectators. They had various ideas as to whom he really was. Jesus asked his disciples, "Who do people say the son of man is?" They replied, "Some say John the Baptist, others say Elijah and others, Jeremiah or one of the prophets." Then Jesus asked, "Who do you say I am?" That's when Simon Peter stepped up to the plate and answered, "You are the Christ, the Son of the living God!" Jesus replied, "Blessed are you, for this was not revealed to you by man, but by my Father in heaven." In baseball language, it can be said that Peter was more than a spectator, he was an ardent fan!

I live in Texas where we have the Texas Rangers in the Dallas-Fort Worth area and for those of us who live on Lake Conroe, we have the Houston Astros. I root for both of these Texas teams as a spectator, but way down deep in my heart, I am "Dodger Blue." As far as I am concerned, that's the difference between a spectator and a real fan.

At every game, fans come equipped with gloves and nets, anticipating this will be the day they snare a foul ball. With hopes as big as their oversized gloves, kids eagerly come early to stake out a claim to snag a foul ball during batting practice. Trying to catch a ball allows an adult to be a kid again. Taking home a ball as a souvenir is a grandstand tradition.

July 6, 2010, in Texas Stadium, a Texas Ranger fan, Tyler Morris, fell from the upper deck to the club level section thirty feet below, while attempting to catch a foul ball. A witness said Morris turned around and leaned back to catch the ball. It had caromed, causing him to loose his balance and flip backward over the rail. He landed on four fans who were not seriously injured. Morris was taken to the hospital with a concussion and sprained ankle. "By the grace of God, no one got seriously hurt," said a fan who sat just past the overhang of the second deck.

Cleveland Indians left fielder, Trevor Crowe, said, "It's one of the scariest things I've seen. All I could think about was to start praying for the guy." So in the outfield, Crowe got on his knees and did just that - he prayed!

The next morning, in the hospital, Morris got his souvenir autographed baseball from Nolen Ryan, Hall of Fame pitcher and president of the Rangers. He also received a bat from his favorite Ranger, outfielder Josh Hamilton.

It is interesting to note, that before the 1920's, fans were required to return balls that landed in the stands. In 1900 a baseball cost three dollars, which is about sixty-five dollars in today's money. Later, when clean white balls became the rule and the cost was not prohibitive, fans were allowed to keep foul balls.

A few years ago, fans began pressuring spectators, who caught a home run ball hit by the visiting club, to throw it back onto the playing field, to show their displeasure. Frankly, it's not a good idea and I hope it will not become a negative tradition.

On September 23, 2009, I was watching the Houston Astros and Cincinnati Reds game on television. The camera followed a foul ball back into the upper deck behind home plate. A young father, sitting in the first row with his three year old daughter, caught the ball. In his delight, at snagging his trophy, he proudly showed it to her. She reached out her little hands for it. Receiving the treasure, she immediately threw her father's prized possession over the barricade and onto the field. His face showed complete surprise and shock, but the next moment he lovingly picked up his little daughter and hugged her with a great adoring smile. It was a precious moment.

The television stations across the country picked it up and showed it time after time. It touched the heartstrings! The entire scene reminded me instantly of Jesus, when he opened his arms to the little ones and said, "Bring the little children to me for of such is the Kingdom of God."

Fielders are allowed to reach into the stands to catch a foul ball. On the other hand, spectators are under no obligation to get out of a fielder's way, when he is attempting to go after the ball. But a spectator is interfering, when he reaches beyond the stands onto the playing field.

When a baseball flies off a bat into the stands, it's a fan's delight when he catches or grabs it. The ball is such a treasured possession; the crowd enjoys sharing one's grand prize. High five's, hugs and cheers are received. Sometimes a struggle occurs in the scramble for the loose ball among the seats.

Returning home with a souvenir ball and a story can also lead to utter chaos. Take the case of a Chicago Cubs avid fan, 26 year-old business man, Steve Bartman. During a vital 2003, National League Championship Series, between the Chicago Cubs and the Florida Marlins, played at the Cubs' Wrigley Field, a foul ball caused great anger and near riot among the Chicago faithful. Steve and other spectators attempted to catch a foul ball, hit by a Marlin batter. At the same time Moises Alou, outfielder for the Cubs, reached into the stands to catch it, but could not glove the ball for the distractions. No rule was broken, because the ball had clearly crossed over into the stands.

Angry Cubs fans became frustrated, realizing that the missed catch could cost the home team the game. The hostility was so heated, Bartman had to be escorted from the stadium by security for his own protection, as he was shouted down with threats and profanities. The fans continued to be irate, for if Alou had made the catch, it looked like a sure win for the Cubbies to clinch the pennant. As it turned out the Cubs team fell apart and lost the game, and later the pennant. Then, they grudgingly watched the Florida Marlins win the World Series.

The saga continued as the ball was finally retrieved by a Chicago lawyer, who sold it for $113,824 to The Harry Carey's restaurant group. On February 26, 2004, the restaurant people ceremoniously exploded the ball into small bits, as Cubs fans watched approvingly. The frustrated fans were somewhat abated.

It is a fact; no team in the pros packs the ball park like the Chicago Cubs fans. Come rain or shine, freezing temperature or howling winds, those jam packed faithful fans sit shoulder to shoulder.

My son Bruce, grandson Conner and I went to a game at Wrigley Field one sunny April afternoon. But after two innings, a late winter blitz of freezing wind came off Lake Michigan and headed straight into Wrigley. To my surprise, those faithful fans were prepared to stay the full nine innings, pulling out their parkas and blankets, ready to endure to the very end. Without a doubt, they were true Cubbie fans. Me? I was freezing! Finally, refuge was found in a stadium restaurant where we watched the game on television. I had been spoiled by Houston's Minute Maid covered stadium.

The New York Mets, from their infancy through eight years of being inept, surprised all sports followers to become the World Series Champions in 1969. They were managed by former Dodger, Gill Hodges. During those struggling, losing years, they still had believing fans who adored them. These fans had to be in the faith category. They had a belief beyond all reason, led by one of their pitchers, Tug McGraw. The homemade banners sprinkled throughout the stadium spelled it out, "You gotta' believe!" It was a positive, catchy theme that hedged on being superstitious, but superstitions often travel with the game.

Carl Erskine in his inside baseball book, *Tales from the Dodger Dugout,* so aptly states, "Baseball is shot through with superstitions. Players, managers and fans all get caught up at one time or another, believing that where they sit, what they wear, or what is said affects the outcome of the game." As for me a Bible believer, I take Faith any day over superstious luck! Superstition is like luck; neither has power of any kind, but it is amazing how people hang on to them.

In Dave Dravecky's book "called up" the San Francisco's heroic pitcher stated, "After I became a Christian, I knew that God was bigger than luck. I could trust Him for the outcome which freed my mind mentally. It sure was easier suiting up before a game without worrying whether today was my "lucky day."

New York Mets manager Bobby Valentine was asked by a reporter if he believed a player can be "jinxed". His reply was almost comical, "I don't believe in superstitions, they're bad luck!"

Superstitions

Well, I'm not superstitious.
Not me. No, not a bit.
But now I's better kiss my bat:
It's almost time to hit.
Gene Fehler

It's a lot of fun to get intensely involved, but to make baseball a religion is to miss the reason for the season. After all, baseball is only a game. I personally share their passion, for I know it's not a game of neutrality.

The Major Leagues All Star baseball game, played in the middle of July every year, leaves me a little flat. It has a lot of hype and is an All-Star feather in the cap for the players, but the intensity is gone. The outcome of who wins or loses is immaterial except the winners get to host the opening of the World Series. It's a neutral game. There are many great players, but really no teams. President Herbert Hoover said, "I enjoy a game much more when I pick a team to win."

The MLB commissioner, Robert Manfred is messing with the purity of baseball when he pulled the 2021 all-star game out of Atlanta over a new Georgia law. Players are not to be pawns in the hands of the powerful. MLB has hit a foul ball! MLB's extra inning rule giving each team a runner on second base to start the inning is a soft corruption to the purity of the game.

This year's all-star game comes with new excitement since the first one played in 1933 at Chicago's Comiskey Park when the American League defeated the national league 4–2. Babe Ruth was the excitement then, as he drove in 2 runs with a third-inning home run with one on board.

The 2021 excitement was in the presence of Los Angeles Angels Japanese star hitter and pitcher Shohei Ohtani. This phenom who leads the majors in home runs is on track to be the Babe Ruth sensation. As "the Babe" saved baseball from the 1919 World series scandal so Ohtani may just do the same thing overshadowing the 2019-2020 Houston Astros cheating shame. It's ironic that four Houston players refused to play in the All-Stars game this year.

A special nice touch at the 2021 All-star game was the wearing of number 44 for the great home run true leader Hank Aaron. Hank passed away this year at the age of 86. A tribute to a great baseball player and a fine man.

As baseball fans crowd around their favorite heroes, so the multitudes followed Jesus with the same adoration. They couldn't get enough of his teaching; he was different. Jesus didn't talk like a Pharisee, Sadducee or other religious leaders. He talked in everyday language telling little stories, "parables" and the people loved it. "Never has anyone ever talked to us this way," is what those in the crowd told the religious leaders. He didn't use big theological terms that no one could understand. He gave the crowd "pocket change words" they could use in every day life; simple words like "ask, seek and knock." Feelings about Jesus were never neutral!

When I was pastor of Tower Grove Baptist Church in St. Louis, Missouri, the enthusiasm for the Cardinals was almost unanimous among the congregation. At the close of the worship service, as I would traditionally stand at the door to shake hands, one older man would usually say, in a low voice, "Pray for the Cardinals." His request would make me chuckle.

To some, baseball is church and they feel God has a favorite team. But does he even care about baseball? I do know that he personally cares about those who play the game. I have always liked what Grantland Rice so eloquently stated, "It's not whether you win or lose, but how you play the game." I can whole-heartedly say "A-men" to that!

When I pitched, I never asked God for a win; I only asked him to help me do my best. Of course, I felt if I did my best, it would be enough to win. But in all seriousness, God is no respecter of persons or team affiliation. As much as I love baseball it was not created in heaven. I do appreciate the old church joke, saying, God was referring to baseball in Genesis 1:1, "In the beginning (big inning) God created the heavens and the earth." But to make baseball more than an athletic contest, is to swing and miss the ball.

It was Father's Day, 1964, when the Phillies' Jim Bunning, a father of seven, took to the mound against the Mets. Ninety pitches later, Bunning had struck out ten and allowed no one to reach first base. Twenty-seven up! and Twenty-seven down! It was the first perfect game in eighty-six years in the National League and the finest hour of the Hall of Famer's baseball career. Bunning's feat was a great tribute for families.

Twelve baseball players from Evangel University of Springfield, Missouri, went on a mission trip to Tlaquepaque, Mexico, for a week in May of 2010. They taught kids baseball as they witnessed to them about Jesus and the Bible. Twin boys, Seth, a catcher, and his brother, Storm, a center fielder, showed their enthusiasm for the mission project by waiting tables at a restaurant in Branson, Missouri, to earn money for the trip. The Evangel team plays in the Heart of America Conference.

Pastor Rick Warren, author of the best seller, *The Purpose Driven Life,* and pastor of the Saddleback Church in Orange County, California, is a terrific baseball fan. In celebration of the mega church's thirtieth year (1980-2010), Pastor Rick led his congregation to lease the Los Angeles Angels baseball stadium for Saturday and Sunday Easter worship services. He delivered his message, "Sermon on the Mound" to the 41,000 weekend worshippers from the Angels' pitchers mound.

I was pleased when Rick called me to send my book" Baseball's sermon on the mound." As his guests Joyce and I flew from Houston to Los Angeles to be present and introduced to his people from the pitcher's mound. A moment to be remembered!

A day at the ball park is one of the finest entertainments a family can enjoy, so after church, let's all go to the ball game!

<blockquote>
Oh, come, come, come, come,
Come to the church in the wildwood
Oh, come to the church in the vale;
No spot is so dear to my childhood
As the little brown church in the vale.
Dr. William S. Pitts
</blockquote>

"I was glad when they said unto me; Let us
go into the house of the Lord."
Psalm 122:1

My grandson "Chief" Chandler Boyles at age eight
pitching in Little League in Castle Rock, Colorado

CHAPTER 3

KID'S STUFF

The Greatest

Little Boy, in a baseball hat
Stands in the field with his ball and bat
Says I am the greatest player of them all
Puts his bat on his shoulder and he tosses up his ball
Don Schlitz
Sung by Kenny Rogers (1999)

BOTTOM OF THE eighth, a line drive to right field and Billy slides into second base, elbow first. Oh, and the crowd hears the "pop" as his arm hits the base. The only thing worse than the pain, was knowing he'd miss the rest of the season. Fortunately, dad was right there for Billy and Columbia Bellaire Medical Center was right around the corner for both of them. An x- ray gave the doctors the exact location of the fracture. After the nurses and doctors signed Billy's cast, he gave them all an autographed baseball. Who knows? It might be priceless after the 2030 World Series?

Earl Weaver, who managed baseball teams for twenty-six years, including the Baltimore Orioles, was right on target when he quipped, "The parent of a little leaguer at a ballgame is simply a nervous breakdown divided into five innings."

Parents and grandparents love kid's baseball. There is probably as much or more excitement in the stands as on the field. While visiting my daughter, Lesli and family in Colorado, I went to my eight-year-old grandson's ball practice. This was "Chief" Chandler's first year to play on a real team with a Tiger's uniform, hat and all. His coach was trying his best to show Chandler how to pitch from the mound. As an old ex-pro pitcher, I watched nervously from the sidelines, trying to keep from correcting the coach's poor technique. Each time my grandson wound up as the coach instructed him, he would lose his balance as he threw the ball. Try as he would, he never threw the ball the entire forty-five feet to the catcher behind home plate. The ball always bounced about five feet short. Chandler was so involved with his coach's instruction about his wind up, he could never get it right.

Finally, I just couldn't stand it any longer, so with a loud voice I hollered, "Chief, throw it over the back stop!" Later, as we drove home my eager little leaguer astounded me, when he leaned against my shoulder and asked, "Grandpa, what's a back stop?"

Little League Baseball, Inc. was organized in the 1939 where the first little league game was played in Williamsport, Pennsylvania. Today it is the largest youth baseball organization in the world. Little League is in eighty-two countries with three million boys and girls from eight to fifteen. Thousands more, play in other youth leagues such as Babe Ruth, Dixie Baseball and Pony League. Each little league team wears uniforms, identical to the Major League team for which they are named. Coaches are urged to teach sportsmanship, teamwork and, of course, baseball skills. The Little League World Series began in 1954, is played every summer in Williamsport, Pennsylvania and viewed by millions on television. In a recent poll among school aged children, baseball was ranked the most popular sport.

Baseball is for girls too. My wife and I were watching the Little League World series on TV when we noticed braids coming from the catcher's mask. Sure enough it was a girl behind the mask and she was doing a great job.

We found she was Ella Bruning from Abilene, Texas. Ella had several brothers and a coach father so it was rather rational for her to play baseball with her brothers. She is the 20th girl to play in the LLWS.

In the texas 6-0 win over Washington she stole second, scored the first run and led the team with two hits and a RBI and took a foul tip on the knee!

At a Willis, Texas elementary school, second- graders are taught once a year; how baseball is related to the subjects they study daily.

Willis High school baseball players in uniform come to the classroom and share in a question-and-answer time. Then the players take the eighty-five or so students outside to measure the distance between bases (math), study the baseball park (geography) and then write letters to their favorite baseball teams or players (language arts).

Instruction

Hitch up her pants, miss her shoulder
With a stream of spit, bump
Her fist into her catcher's mitt,
And stare incredulously at the ump.
Conrad Hilberry

Seniorific news gives the baseball history of 90 year old Donna Roberts. She was among the 600 female baseball players in the all-American Girls Professional Baseball league founded in 1943 by Chicago Cubs own Phillip K. Wrigley, as a means of keeping baseball parks in business while team's male players were drafted to fight in the war.

Roberts played shortstop. "I really could catch any fly that came our way. I don't remember missing any" She said, now living in hometown Billings, Montana, "once we got through playing a game, the little girls would come out on the field and ask for autographs."

I learned how to pitch," seven year old Sabrian Thomas said. "They also taught us how to run to first base, then second base, then third base and finally home." Sabrian plans to play on a baseball team when she gets older. "You just got to try your best," she told Kassia Micek, *The Courier of Montgomery County, Texas,* staff writer.

The second grade teacher, Jana Edginton, a Los Angles Dodgers fan concluded, "The kids have such a great time learning how to incorporate every day things with baseball." At the end of the session, students received autographed baseballs from the high school ball players, which made it a grand slam day.

While visiting my daughter, Lisa and family, in Quito, Ecuador, I helped my granddaughter, Gloria, celebrate her seventh birthday. Her party was a princess affair. Gloria and her friends were dressed in "high society" garb, their hair done up and entirely too much make-up. The girls wore trendy high heeled shoes and their mom's jewelry. It was a little girl's party par excellence!

When she opened her presents, my gift brought puzzled looks from the guests, but not from Gloria. Grandpa's present was a purple leather baseball glove! To Gloria it was a matter-of-fact gift. After all, grandpa did play for the Dodgers!

Church leagues for kids are rather common in Texas. While I was pastor of the Southcliff Baptist church in Fort Worth, we had a church team in The Royal Ambassador League for children, ages eight to eleven. Praying before every game was a common practice and incidentally, we won every game!

Tee ball starts with four year olds who never face a pitcher, but hit a ball sitting on a plastic pole. It's a good start for children.

It doesn't matter whether you are on a team or not, any boy or girl, who holds a ball has an instinct to throw it. If they put their fingers around a stick of wood, somehow there is a desire to hit something. When they see a ball rolling on the ground or moving in the air, there is an urge to catch it. It's just human nature. So any kid can play and have fun anywhere. Baseball goes far beyond a little leaguer's desire to play. It's often quoted, "In every real man a child is hidden who wants to play." Playing ball is fun for every kid, whether it's on the front lawn, back yard, down at a school ground, in a park, or an empty lot.

When my twin and I were eleven, we did baseball in our front yard. We played with a fair-sized rock and took turns batting with an old broom stick. That didn't last long. One day our neighbor, Mr. Dorey, came over and gave us a ball and a black bat and suggested that we go down to the school yard to play. I think he was more concerned for the windows of his house than our safety.

During my first year at Dodgertown, the outstanding catcher was Roy Campanella. "Campy" had a big smile for everyone, even during those hot, humid morning practice sessions, when he caught pitchers in the "strings" area. He is quoted in *Uncle John's Reader*, "You've got'ta be a man to play baseball for a living, but you got'ta have a lot of little boy in you, too." I can still see "Campy" smiling through his mask.

Baseball historian, George Vescey, wrote it right, "The sport has a timeless feel to it." The hilarious comedy act of the 1930's with Bud

Abbott and Lou Costello trying to figure out "Who's on First," still brings laughter to everyone. It's a kids' game that grows up with us.

Fred and I loved to play baseball at our neighborhood school yard. We had one problem though; neither of us owned a glove, so when we played a pick- up game we had to borrow gloves from our buddies. But, we twins had a double-trouble problem; we were both left handed. The gloves we borrowed, unfortunately, were for right handers. Some of the kids called us "wrong- handers."

It was a little tricky, for us to maneuver a right-handed glove, but we soon learned how: catch the ball, toss it and the glove in the air, re-catch the ball and throw. We lost only a moment in the transfer and got pretty good at it!

I think we were inspired by Pete Gray, a one armed outfielder for the St. Louis Browns. He played during World War II, when many of the major leaguers were in the military. Pete caught the ball with his only hand, threw the ball and glove in the air, caught the tossed ball and threw it toward the infield with amazing quickness. Gray actually hit five home runs with his one arm swings. I always admired him for achieving excellence in spite of his handicap.

In 1945, when we were eleven years old, we were playing baseball in the schoolyard. Our grandfather Minton drove up and stopped his old black Model A Ford in the middle of the street. "Hey, Frank and Fred!" he hollered from the open window. Then he threw two boxes in the street and immediately drove off. Puzzled, we raced to the boxes. Man, were we thrilled when we opened them and found two brand new left-handed leather baseball gloves! Now, for the first time, we could play baseball like the other boys. Our baseball careers were on track.

Excerpts from Dan Liberthson's poem, *Mitt*, brings into focus the happiness we received with our new gloves.

Mitt

Ever since my first real mitt
I've loved the smell of leather,
Smell that is a feel,
so rich and thick it is (. . .)
when I wore my mitt

I changed, like Clark Kent,
into a thing more potent
than a spindly boy. (…)

Baseball belongs to the family. It's PG rated entertainment at every game and lasts all season. During World War II many of the finest ball players left baseball to defend our country. Baseball officials and owners considered cancelling play until the war was over. However, President Roosevelt appealed to them to continue the games, because he knew the positive impact it had on the nation. He also realized that the strength of the nation was in the family structure and baseball was a family affair. His thoughts were, "The tie that binds families also binds the nation."

Jesus always endeared himself to family. He performed his first miracle at a home wedding in Nazareth, when he turned water into wine. Later, at a festival a crowd demanded, "Where is your family?" He surprised them by saying, "Whoever does the will of God, are my brothers and sisters and mother." That spells family!

Baseball teams are like family. Teams that are together in mind and desire are winners. Players' friendships go far beyond the field of play. When Mickey Mantle lay in the hospital dying, he called for his Christian teammate, Bobby Richardson, to come and be by his side. They talked of the Kingdom of God and life and death. Praying together, Mickey gave his heart to the Lord Jesus.

John McClusky's baseball prose, found on the internet, *Baseball Almanac,* is a personal account of his father taking him to his first baseball game.

"Moments I shall never forget!

Your father got the tickets. Tonight. You still can't believe it, though you're sitting in the front seat of the Chevy with him, on a warm June evening…… But it's true. You're going to your first ballgame. Tonight. . . And you're inside at last…… The excited voices……The buying of a quick hot dog and soda. Peanuts, too, of course….And soon you're sitting down…….The night air chills you, so you slip on the jacket mom made you bring and you sit and cheer with your father. And you love him more than you ever did. Here, watching the White Sox together……. You yell and hoot, your father laughs with pleasure and you love him even more than ever...... Yes, you love him. Here and now, in Comiskey Park."

Home is the centerpiece of baseball. It is at home plate where the game starts, when the ump calls, "Play Ball!" The bases form a diamond that is the path to home. After the batter hits the ball he runs counter clock wise, touching all three bases on the way to home. The strongest play in baseball is the home run. Who hasn't felt the thrill of sliding across home plate through swirling dust, to hear the umpire ring out, "Safe, safe at home!" Baseball tugs at the heart of home and family.

Yankee Mariano Rivera, at forty, was one of the greatest relief pitchers in history. He was interviewed in October 2009 by Tom Verducci of *Sports Illustrated,* just before the New York Yankees headed to the playoffs of the American league. The reporter brought up the respect that Mario gives to his baseball peers. He said, "I don't wait for people to give me respect, I always give them respect, any player, even a rookie, an old player, a veteran. I never try to show up anybody." He went on to say, "It comes from back home, family. My father taught me no matter who it is, every body is an uncle." Then this outstanding pitcher concluded, "To me, everybody was someone I respect, like family. I grew up that way."

One of my favorite memories of family and baseball, was lying on a mattress we placed on our living room floor on hot summer nights. Our house had no air conditioning, so we opened the windows and front door to let the breeze blow through. Then, we would listen to the radio broadcast of the National Baseball Congress Semipro Tournament. These games had been played in Lawrence-Dumont Stadium in Wichita, Kansas every year since 1931. Teams as far away as Fairbanks, Alaska and Melbourne Beach, Florida competed for the prize of being the national semipro champion. The schedule is tight. Game after game is played all day and then, far into the night, often spilling over into the early morning hours. Our dad, Fred, and I would lie there and listen in the friendly darkness until one-by-one we dropped off to sleep. It is such a good close family memory.

My twin, Fred, who spent three years as an outfielder in the Brooklyn Dodger and Baltimore Orioles baseball organizations, wrote this heart warming poem in 1977, just after our father passed away.

Two Over Here!
(The Day They Tore down the old ballpark)

Today they scooped away the old ball field
The score board goes tomorrow.
A big new store will cover the place
Where losing games brought sorrow.
I sadly watched from bleacher seats
The ones I sat with dad.
But the glad memories of the past
Overshadowed this day so sad.
Dad taught me the "grand old game"
From those old bleacher seats
Stories galore that I heard
Brought ever so fast heartbeats.
"Hot dogs, peanuts, get 'em here!"
My dad yelled "Two over here!"
I miss his smile as I miss this place
I miss those days and miss his face.
Second base is gone…it didn't take long
Third base was a cinch
The visitor's dugout is gone …the pitcher's mound
And the left field bullpen bench.
I saw it all go…the big grandstand
The home dugout…the tall flag pole
That old green fence…where kids peeked in
That famous old knot hole.
Well, Dad is gone…the players gone
A big store soon will win this race.
"Two over here…Two over here!"
I miss Dad's yell, as I miss this place.
Fred D. Minton, Ph.D.

Kids do make a difference. Baseball was a kid's game before it became an adult sport. It became popular among the soldiers during America's tragic Civil War. Then it spread all over the country when the troops came home. In almost every town, former soldiers organized baseball teams.

Fortunate are the teen bat boys who, are posted near the dugouts and the ball boys and girls as they sit along the side lines retrieving the fouls. Bat boys get the bats ready for the hitter and are a real help to the home plate umpire, delivering the needed balls at his call. They are doing jobs that many kids only dream about. Players enjoy the friendship of kids who help out on the field during the games. It is awesome for these kids to be next to celebrated players.

I was watching the 2002 World Series game on television, in my home on Lake Conroe in Montgomery, Texas, when I saw a little bat boy going toward home plate, while the game was in play. I couldn't figure it out at the time, but later, the announcer gave us word that he was the son of San Francisco Giants manager, Dusty Baker. The three and a half year old boy went out to get a bat while the play was still going on. Giants player, J.T. Snow, grabbed the little guy at home plate while still in the middle of scoring his run. This saved the bat boy from a possible collision with runners behind him or players from the Los Angeles Angels. Immediately, Major League Baseball set the minimum age of fourteen for bat boys.

Eric Nielsen, retired oil executive told me at the Sugar Creek Baptist Church, the story of his boyhood friend, Frank McNulty, who was a Boston Braves bat boy in the 1940's. Frank was fourteen when he was the live model for the Norman Rockwell painting of a bat boy. The painting appeared on the cover of *The Saturday Evening Post*, May 23, 1948. In December 2009, it was sold at auction in New York for $662,500. Ironically, McNulty was in a Chicago Cubs bat boy uniform and not his regular one of the Boston Braves. McNulty now 78, lives in Sea Brook Island, South Carolina and is the retired editor of the popular, *Parade Magazine.*

Another old time bat boy, who lived to be over one hundred, is Authur Gidden. His duties in 1923, at age fourteen, "were shining shoes, collecting bats, chasing balls and 'chugging' milk." He told *Bygone Baseball Magazine,* reporter, "It would be wonderful to be a bat boy again."

While in the batter's circle, waiting for my turn at the plate, I enjoyed the friendship of the bat boys. Usually I was on one knee while I waited and that gave me a chance to talk with them. That's when I could say a few words about church or Jesus, before I went to bat.

Years later, when I was traveling to a speaking engagement, I stopped to gas up my car. When I gave my credit card to the young attendant, he gave me a big smile and said, "Minton, I was your bat boy when you played with the Dodger team in Shawnee, Oklahoma. I'm going to the University of Oklahoma now and I'm a member of the First Baptist Church, too. I remember you always talked with me about the Lord before you went to bat." For me, that was a heart warmer.

In 1946, Little League had yet to be organized, in Wichita, Kansas area, so our leagues were formed by the American Legion organization. All teams were sponsored by businesses that furnished the equipment and usually chose the manager. The kids were invited to play with the manager's approval. Playing on a real team was a step up from school yard play.

One day, as we were playing in a school yard pick-up game my twin, Fred, caught a fly ball over his shoulder. For an eleven year old, it was a sensational catch! Some of the boys, who were on an official team, gathered around us and said, "Hey, you guys are pretty good! How would you like to play on a real team?"

We all trooped over to our house. Mom was sitting on the porch swing and several of the guys almost in unison, blurted out, "Mrs. Minton, can Frank and Fred try out for our team?" Mom, who could always say no before yes, surprised us with a big "Yes!" Happily, our baseball careers were under way!

Belonging to a team was one of the warmest feelings of my child hood. I still remember my first uniform. It proved I belonged. The letters across the white jersey in red and blue spelled *U Select It*. This was the name of the sponsoring company, who manufactured automatic candy dispensing machines. They furnished uniforms, all of the baseball equipment plus the manager. I trembled with excitement as I stretched my legs into the pants. Proudly, I put on my jersey, pulled up my stockings, got into my shoes, placed my cap on my head and suddenly I was on my way to the Majors. I walked to the mirror to see myself. I was eleven and proud as punch at what I saw! I had been transformed from a mere boy into a real ballplayer!

There was excitement and anticipation in the air when I got to the ball field and saw my teammates in our uniforms. I only knew a few of them but immediately I could tell, "Hey, that's my team!" I felt secure that I was one of them and I immediately bonded.

Uniforms have always been an essential part of the game and have held deep significance for fans. Spectators give "high fives" to complete strangers because they are both wearing shirts of the same team. It is as if they belong to the same family.

The first team uniform was the 1849 New York City Knickerbockers baseball club. It consisted of a white flannel shirt, blue wool pants and a straw hat. The Knickerbockers were more of a social club than an athletic group; their attire on the field was more for style than play. Since baseball was a gentleman's game, style was more important. Yet, throughout more than 160 years of baseball, those original uniforms have a continuing influence, except for the straw hats.

The straw-hats didn't last. Soon a stubby new model was designed to keep the sun out of the players eyes. Then in 1901, the Detroit Tigers made the innovation of putting their namesake tiger on their caps

Smithsonian Magazine states, "Perhaps America's greatest fashion export is the baseball cap, it changed the way people dress in every country. The world tips the hat to baseball!

In early days baseball teams wore knee pants similar to a cricket uniform. The uniforms were drab and looked similar, which made the color of the stockings the distinctive factor in identifying a team. That's why early teams picked up nicknames, such as, Chicago White Sox, Boston Red Sox, St. Louis Browns and the Cincinnati Red Stockings, who are now the Reds.

Hang on to your old baseball uniform and don't get rid of it. It's a historic relic. Shocking, but true, in 1954, when the Baltimore Orioles bought the franchise of the hapless Browns, the new owner threw the old Browns uniforms into the street! What a treasure they would be today.

I still have my road uniform from when I pitched for the Dodger farm team in 1955. It's the real McCoy. When the Dodgers Major League team got new uniforms, the old ones were sent to an affiliated minor league club. Mine is one of those hand-me-downs, traditional light gray, 100% wool with the familiar Dodger blue scripted logo on the shirt and a blue number 47 on the back. I still have those matching blue wool stockings, with several moth holes.

Did Jesus and his disciples wear any special type of clothing? The Bible does not indicate that they did. One must assume he wore the typical clothing of the day. A popular novel and movie in the late 40's, *The Robe,* gave the impression that the robe of Jesus had special power.

It is interesting that after Jesus was crucified four soldiers divided his clothing among themselves but cast lots for his underclothing that was seamless woven in a one piece from top to bottom.

The Bible tells of a woman, who had a life of physical suffering. She reached out from the crowd, and touched the hem of Jesus' garment. "If I can touch his clothes, I will be healed," she thought. Immediately, she was healed! At once Jesus realized that power had gone out from him. He turned around in the crowd and asked, 'Who touched my clothes'?" His disciples said, "You see the people crowding around you and yet you ask, 'who touched me'?" But Jesus kept looking around to see who had done it. Then the woman fell at his feet and told him the whole truth. He said to her, "Daughter, your faith has healed you." It was Jesus' power and her faith that brought the healing. The Bible reveals that the power came from Jesus and not his clothing.

What makes a ball player? Is it the uniform he wears? The Dodger Blue or the Yankee pin strip does not a ball player make. I remember when a fresh rookie, just out of college, was in the hotel lobby wearing our team's ball cap. Our manager, "Little Buffalo" Perry said, "Show 'em you're a ball player on the field, son, not in the hotel lobby!"

When I was a boy, wearing my first uniform didn't make me a ball player. That first year was a real learning experience. I was so confused at times. If it weren't for my manager, who cared more for kids than winning, I might have quit out of discouragement. Dropped balls, overthrows, and strike outs were my kind of game. But that didn't matter, baseball fever had struck!

For three summers my brother and I took the bus to downtown Wichita, transferred to another, going across town to the East High School diamonds, to play the game we loved. Baseball had become our magnificent obsession. All the while, I was learning baseball and improving in a big way. The dream of being a professional continued to drive me on. "Some day, somewhere, I'll be one of them."

Dan Liberthson knew the heart of a boy and he picked it up in this poem.

Batboy

<blockquote>
When I grow up
I want to be just like them.
I don't care if they lose
though I'd rather be
them when they win.
</blockquote>

When does a boy become part of his dream? In baseball, he might have to wait a while, but in God's work it can be right now.

One day Jesus and the disciples had a real problem. Thousands had come to hear Him speak in an open field in Galilee. As the day wore on the crowd became restless with hunger. There were no food supplies near, but Jesus in his masterful way seemed concerned, but not worried.

About that time Andrew, Simon Peter's brother, brought a boy to Jesus. The boy had five small loaves of bread and two fish and was willing to share all that he had. To the amazement of those 5,000 gathered on the hillside, Jesus blessed the food and it multiplied over and over until all were fed. Later Jesus said, "I am the bread of life."

In 1992 while visiting my daughter Lisa and family in London, England, I took my nine year old grandson, Pepe, to the world famous Hyde Park. On the Green, we found a pick-up baseball game of British and American teens. It wasn't long before my Pepe begged them to let him play. Some of the guys laughed at the very idea of this little boy playing, but they relented.

They had no idea who they were up against. I had taught my grandson some old pro tricks on how to swing a bat and slug the ball. When Pepe came to bat, all the teens moved closer to home plate. Wow, were they surprised! Pepe slugged that ball over their heads and motored around the sacks for a solid triple! It was a grand and glorious afternoon in Hyde Park.

In 1971, I was asked by Southern Baptist missionary, Dr. Roy Lyon, to hold some baseball clinics in Venezuela, South America. I was then pastor of the Southcliff Baptist Church of Fort Worth, Texas and fourteen years removed from my minor league playing days. I was grateful that the Southcliff congregation was very supportive in sending their baseball preacher on a seventeen day missionary trip. I packed boxes of Spanish New Testaments and my old number 47 Dodger uniform and off I went, once again, to play ball!

I traveled to the great city of Caracas and seven other towns and villages throughout Venezuela. I found ball fields everywhere I went, even in the jungle villages. If you think that only American kids love baseball, you should have been with me and experienced the enthusiasm of those South Americans. When we held a clinic, we found the ball fields crowded with eager, excited kids. In one small town even the mayor came and demonstrated his pitching ability.

Hundreds of boys came out of the rural jungled areas with enthusiasm to play baseball. The missionary told me, "In all of my twenty years of mission work these baseball events have been the best response I have ever seen."

The boys were always eager to have my signature so after the clinic was over I signed my name on the front page of the free Spainish New Testaments that were handed out. In one little village as the boys huddled around me for my autograph, I pointed to the missionary who was on one knee unboxing the New Testaments I exclaimed "Go get one and I'll sign it!"

Those fifty or more baseballer's took off runing like a herd of buffaloes toward the poor unsuspecting missionary. Down to the ground he went pumpeled by those Bible snatching excited kids and then off they ran to me as I stood, astounded!

With a big smile on his face, Dr. Lyon hollered to me, "I've never seen any group, anywhere so excited to get a Bible!"

During that time, South America had adopted a favorite son of international baseball fame, Roberto Clemente, who was from Puerto Rico. He was a dominant outfielder for the Pittsburg Pirates from 1955 to 1972. Wherever I went, I fielded question after question about their hero. His great hitting and fielding in the 1971 World Series made him the most talked about athlete in the world. Speaking through my missionary interpreter, those Venezuelan little leaguers were enthralled when I told about Clemente. For them, it was like reaching out and touching the "hem of his baseball garment."

On the final day of the 1972 regular season, Clemente had collected his 3,000th hit, but he didn't take time to celebrate this historical mark. Learning of a terrible earthquake in Nicaragua and the subsequent plight of his adopted country, Roberto immediately made preparations for a mercy flight. We were shocked and saddened by news reports that Clemente was killed in the crash of the mercy plane carrying relief supplies to Managua, Nicaragua. His sudden death and heartfelt generosity touched the world.

The following year, he was rightfully voted into the Hall of Fame. The mandatory five year waiting period was waived for only the second time in baseball history. The only other time was for the great Lou Gehrig.

The following poem was written by Juan A. Perez in memory of Roberto Clemente. He died on New Year's Eve at thirty-eight while on the mission trip to help the victims of an earthquake in Nicaragua.

The Game's True Leaders

There is a town
Down by the sea
Where grown men cry
On new year's eve.

There is an exciting event in the book of Acts concerning a boy who placed himself in harm's way to help his uncle, the apostle Paul. His age is never revealed in scripture, but in Jewish life a boy of twelve was considered and referred to as a young man. He may have been in Jerusalem to get his schooling as Paul had done years earlier.

The Apostle Paul had been placed under guard in the Roman barracks for his own protection, from a riotous crowd, who had accused him of proclaiming statements against their way of life. The anger of the crowd was so fierce, forty men banded together and committed themselves to neither eat nor drink until they killed Paul. This plan was suicidal, for even a mob was at risk of their lives, if they made an attempt to take a prisoner from Roman guards. Whether they were successful or not, those who lived would have been executed by the Roman government.

Paul's nephew heard of the plot and immediately went to the prison to tell Paul about the terrible plan for him to be killed. Paul sent his nephew straight to the guard. The guard immediately sent him to the Commander, who listened and placed his hand on the boy's shoulder and said, "Tell no one about this." Then, at nine o'clock at night he ordered Paul out of Jerusalem under a detachment of two hundred armed soldiers and seventy horsemen, transferring him safely to Caesarea. The boy's actions were brave and enabled Paul to continue preaching the Gospel.

Baseball heroics not only happen in the Major Leagues but they can occur in kids' games as well. *The Courier of Montgomery County, Texas,* June 5, 2009, carried the story of Seth Heeman of the IOU Conroe, Texas Area Youth Baseball Mariners. He attained one of baseball's most elusive accomplishments on April 16. Seth, a 110 pound right-hander, threw a perfect game. No one from the opposing team reached base and Heeman struck out every batter he faced. Even though Seth had thrown two other no- hitters that season, he was not aware of the distinction between a no-hitter and a perfect game, until it was all over. Heeman said, "I knew no one had gotten' a hit and I was just trying to get 'um all out."

I've Never Written a Baseball Poem

I didn't even make
the seventh grade girl's third team
substitute.
Elisavietta Ritchie

During World War II my dad was a civilian employed by the United States Navy. We lived in a government housing project on the beach in Coronado, California, which was across the bay from San Diego. Our apartment was the end unit, only thirty feet from the beach. We felt fortunate to live in the newly built "projects" on Mullennex Drive. There was a sandy courtyard between the housing units, just large enough for nine and ten year old kids to play. Here is where I learned what "pick-up" baseball was all about; rowdy, loud and unfair. Even my year older, red haired sister, Marliene, got into the game. And yes, here is where I got my first window breaking home run, right through our neighbor's kitchen. You talk about a "walk off hit," this was a "run off," as we scattered in all directions.

To this very day, I have in the trunk of my Lincoln, two baseballs and two gloves, just in case some kid wants to play catch. You never can tell, he might be the next Albert Pujols! I also have a New Testament in the side pocket of my car because, who knows, one of those kids might become the next Billy Graham!

These gloves and Bible also remind me of what Jesus said, "As you go, make disciples." The Bible further admonishes, in baseball jargon, "Be ready, in season and out of season!"

CHAPTER 4

SIGN HIM UP!

You have not chosen me, but I have chosen you.
Jesus

ALMOST EVERY AMERICAN kid has dreamed of being a baseball player at one time or another. Hollywood star, Robert Redford, who was "The Natural" in baseball's greatest film, said when interviewed by the *Wall Street Journal*, "I pitched for the University of Colorado, but when a little boy I always wanted to be a pro ball player." Armand Eisen in his book, *Play Ball!* quotes President Eisenhower, "When I was a small boy growing up in Kansas, a friend of mine and I went fishing ... I told him I wanted to be a real major league baseball player, a genuine professional like Honus Wagner. My friend said that he'd like to be President of the United States, neither of us got our wish."

Just like President Eisenhower, my twin, and I also dreamed of being pro baseball players; but catch was the game before we played on a team. We walked to Waco Avenue School, a short block from our home, where we threw the ball back and forth to each other in all kinds of crazy ways. The distance between us was optional. Sometimes we tossed the ball rapidly up close and at times we would back up and throw long distance. We made a game of counting how many times we could throw it without a miss. We often played until dark.

Catch

High, make him fly off the ground for it,
low, make him stoop,
Make him scoop it up, make him as-almost-as-possible miss it,
Anything, everything tricky, risky, nonchalant,
Anything under the sun to outwit the prosy,
Robert Francis

In the summer, we played catch every day at the school yard for hours. If another kid showed up, we'd play work-up. This game was comprised of a batter, a pitcher and the poor guy who was the outfielder to shag the balls that were hit. If the shagger or the pitcher caught a ball on the fly, they exchanged positions with the batter.

On some occasions a bunch of neighborhood kids would be there, so we would get a pick-up game going. Age or size didn't make any difference, because everyone who showed up was eligible to play. Our school yard rules were flexible, so how many kids or how few, was never a problem.

To choose up sides we used the time honored, "grab the bat, hand over hand method." This was our attempt to be fair. Two players, usually the biggest, were chosen as bat grabbers and were named captains.

The bat was tossed in the air and one captain grabbed the fat end of the bat. The second captain placed his hand just above the first. The captains placed one hand above the other until one hand reached the knob. The captain, who could hold the bat by the knob for even a moment, earned the right of first pick for his team. Back and forth the choosing would go until the last kid was picked. Nobody wanted to be picked last and I mean nobody!

Jesus calls all whether first or last. He said, "You have not chosen me but I have chosen you."

Yet, being picked last was of no consequence to Jesus. He told a story of a farmer who hired laborers early in the morning to work in his vineyard for a denarius. Throughout the day he hired more workers, who worked the remainder of the day, also for a denarius. At the end of the day he gave them their pay, starting with the last hired and ending with the first. So when the first ones came, they assumed they would be paid more. The farmer insisted he paid them what he promised. Jesus concluded, "The last shall be first and the first shall be last." They were all chosen, they were all signed up, and they were all paid fairly. Actually, Jesus was talking about salvation.

Whether you were saved in Vacation Bible School or on a death bed as an older adult the same salvation is given by God in Jesus Christ.

The last being picked was demonstrated very vividly in the life of King David, when he was a boy tending sheep on his father, Jesse's ranch. God had commissioned the prophet Samuel to anoint one of Jesse's eight sons to be the next king. After Samuel saw the first seven sons, he asked "Are these all the sons you have?"

"There is still the youngest," Jesse answered, "but he is tending the sheep." Samuel said, "Send for him." So David was called to the house and was observed. The Lord said to the prophet, "Rise and anoint him; he is the one." Samuel then anointed him as God's choice to be the next king of Israel.

Why did God choose David? The admonition of God was carried out, for "The Lord does not look at the things man looks at, for man looks at the outward appearance, but the Lord looks at the heart." David was the one chosen even though he was last.

It is interesting that David did not become the king immediately. He went right back to the sheepfold. It was ten years after his anointing before he reigned as King of Israel.

The baseball scout tries to look into the future, as he goes about selecting young men to ink a contract with his club. No one really knew what New York Yankee scout, Tom Greenwade, saw in an unknown Oklahoma high school shortstop named Mickey Mantle. Thousands of other high school ballplayers looked as good, but in that seventeen year old, Tom knew immediately he had found greatness. Mickey was signed with a $500 bonus to play for the Yankee class C Joplin, Missouri team in the KOM League. At times Mickey's play was ragged and baseball people held little hope for a major league future for the sandy-haired kid.

Yet, in the next few years, Mickey Mantle was rewriting Yankee history as the brilliant outfielder who took over patrolling center field from New York's icon Joe DiMaggio. It wasn't long before Mickey awed the baseball world as one of the greatest sluggers of all time. Mickey's 565 foot tape-measured homer on April 17, 1953 at old Griffin Stadium in Washington D.C. is still considered the longest on record. In that game Mickey, who was a switch hitter, was batting right handed against left handed pitcher, Chuck Dobbs, of the Washington Senators. Mantle hit a rising line drive that nicked the lower right corner of a huge sign atop a football scoreboard behind the center field bleachers. The ball carried on leaving the stadium and continued in the air across a street, finally landing in someone's yard. The home run's flight caught the imagination of the fans, who began calling such power hits, "tape measure" home runs. With that prowess, the kid from Oklahoma became the Babe Ruth of the 50's and 60's.

Mickey was just four years older than me, when he started his professional baseball career. When Fred and I signed with the Dodgers, he was the young player we really admired. We met Mickey during spring training in 1955. The Yankees had come to Vero Beach for a "grapefruit" game. Word had gotten around; Fred and I were friendly, outgoing Christians. So as a joke, Don Drysdale and some of the guys set us up to meet Yogi Berra and Mickey. We did not know they had been warned that we were out to convert them. When the bus arrived with the Yankee team, we were pushed near the door of the bus. The Yankee players arranged for Yogi and Mickey to be the first ones to get off. When the doors opened, Drysdale yelled, "Here they are!" Yogi did his best to scramble back onto the bus when he spotted us. Both teams erupted in laughter. We had been "had!" But the day wasn't lost. Yogi and Mickey shared dinner with Fred and me in the Dodger dining hall that evening. Throughout the years, Fred and I have laughed about our big rookie moment in spring training, for we knew it was done in fun.

We all prayed for Mickey when we learned of his cancer and need for a liver transplant. It is difficult to realize your hero is going to die. We learned later of his call to his former teammate, Yankee second baseman, Bobby Richardson. Together they talked about salvation in Jesus Christ.

Here's an account of his last days as chronicled in "Mickey Mantle: His Final Inning," by Ed Cheek, published by the American Tract Society.

"Mickey knew he was facing death. During the All-Star break in Dallas, he picked up the phone and called his old friend and teammate, former Yankee second baseman Bobby Richardson - a committed Christian. Mickey asked him to pray for him over the telephone.

A few weeks later when doctors had discovered that the cancer had aggressively spread, Mickey's family asked Bobby if he would come visit him. His death was imminent.

After entering the hospital room, Richardson went over to Mantle's bed and took his hand. Locking his eyes on him, Bobby said, "Mickey, I love you, and I want you to spend eternity in heaven with me." Mantle smiled and said, "Bobby, I've been wanting to tell you that I have trusted Jesus as my Savior." For Richardson, this brought tears to his eyes. For years, he had talked to Mickey about the Lord Jesus, but to no avail. Now, in the final inning of his life, the Mick had won his greatest victory - more glorious than any of his tape-measure home runs."

I am grateful that one day, I will meet my baseball hero in heaven, who became my brother in Christ.

Ball players need to have fun beyond the diamond. Sometimes they go a little overboard. The recent so called, funny act, of smearing the face of the "player of the game" with shaving cream, as he is being interviewed, is crude and absurd. It is not a joke. I find it demeaning and not worthy of baseball's great traditions of honor. Spraying champagne in the club house after a Pennant or World Series win is also suspect.

Joe Kay AP baseball writer in his article, September 27, 2010 "Reds clinch title" wrote, "The reds sold 30,151 tickets for the clinching game and took the field almost tasting it. Second baseman Brandon Phillips said he doesn't drink and has never taken so much as a sip of champagne. Everybody is looking forward to seeing me do it, Phillips said, 'I don't know how it's going to taste. I don't know what's going to happen'." It's not good for a bad tradition to smudge the conviction of a godly man and ball player like Brandon.

Hats off to the 2010 Texas Rangers, American League Pennant Champions, for celebrating on the field by spraying Ginger Ale instead of Champaign. By doing so, the team honored their MVP Josh Hamilton's faith and request. It is well known that Josh is a recovering alcohol and drug abuser.

The Rangers were also acknowledging non-drinking pitcher C.J. Wilson. Wilson's stand came from seeing the problems caused by alcohol and drugs in the lives of family members and peers. It was a clean act by the pennant winners before a happy, cheering home stadium crowd.

I personally know what Josh and C.J. went through for I too had an alcoholic father and an erratic home life. I felt kin to them and their Christian convictions, I can say, I have never tasted an alcoholic beverage and that means beer also. Like they say in Texas, "If it's the truth then you ain't braggin'!" In the minors in the 1950's alcoholic beverages were the toast of our wins. The beer was free, but I had to buy my soft drink to celebrate our victories. It was worth it!

After a winning game in Reno, Nevada in which I pitched a nine inning shutout, a frequent visitor, Billy Exstien, a nationally recognized singer came into the club house to celebrate with us. Noticing I was dressing and not drinking, Billy came over to me, "Hey Minton you're the star, come on and celebrate with us! Its ok, I'm a Baptist too!"

For the first time if I ever wanted a swig of beer, this was the moment. All the guys chimed in, "Come on Minton!"

I knew I wouldn't go to Hell if I drank it but my Christian testimony was on the line. In that pressured moment, I just gave a great big smile and went on dressing. It wasn't easy but I cared for my team mates souls and lives more than a moment of comradeship.

As I left the club house early I remembered what I had read in the Bible, "do not do anything that will make your brother stumble whether eating or drinking."

I didn't know how I was going to be received by the team the next day. But to my surprise, our short stop Charley Smith said, "Minton, I won $10 from Murray on a bet that you wouldn't drink that beer!" The icey reception that I feared melted!

The importance of a good scout to a major league organization cannot be overestimated. The scout holds the future of the club in his hands. He must see more than the fans; more than just runs, hits and errors. He must judge actions, reflexes, intelligence and desire. The scout travels back roads, villages, small towns, inner cities, anywhere he might see a ball game and find another Mickey Mantle or Sandy Koufax.

In 1948, the oldest rookie in history signed with the Cleveland Indians. Pitcher LeRoy "Satchel" Paige was forty-two and had been a star for twenty years in the Negro National League before coming to the majors. That year he was selected "Rookie of the Year!" His comment on aging reflects his wit. "How old would you be if you didn't know how old you was?" He had a windup and swift delivery fastball which kept him in the majors until 1965. Amazingly, at age fifty-nine he pitched three scoreless innings in a major league game for the Kansas City Royals. In 1975, he was inducted into baseball's Hall of Fame.

Satchell, was not only a great ball player, he was entertainingly quotable as Carl Erskine, outstanding Dodger pitcher writes, "He threw a variety of pitches he called 'inshoots, outshoots, risers, and drops; all for strikes!" Eskine continued, "I once talked to Satchel and asked him to describe his best stuff. In his unique way of talking he said, 'Well, Cawl, I had a little piece o' fastball and a little piece o'curve, then a dab o'this and that'."

Even though, the Apostle Peter was the oldest "rookie" of the original disciples, he certainly couldn't have made "rookie of the year." Throughout the time that he followed Jesus, he continued to make mistakes. He confidently stated, "Even though all others would forsake you, I will not." But he did! Another time when Jesus was predicting his own death, Peter blurted out, "Never Lord, this shall never happen to you!" Jesus knew how wrong he was and rebuked him on the spot.

Peter was too much of an earthly rookie, to get the true picture of why Jesus came to earth. It took three entire seasons of following him, before Peter fully understood that Jesus came to die on the Cross, as the sacrificial Lamb of God. Often, we expect too much of our Bible heroes.

The same is true of our expectations of young baseball players. Hunter Pence was a young dynamic outfielder for the Houston Astros. He energized the team with this gazelle like running in the outfield and on the basepaths. But sometimes his daring base running cost the Houston club a rally inning. He frustrated the team and fans with his seemingly inexperience but Houston loved him anyway. He became a leader in his own right. We miss him even to this day as he moved on to become a star with the Los Angeles Angels.

As a baseball scout searches for prospects, his work has become high-tech with laptops, cell phones and blackberries being common tools of the trade. But it is his experience in evaluating ballplayers that makes him worth the investment. Baseball is a sport but it is also a business. A ball club will spend up to 2 million dollars to bring a rookie all the way through the minors to the big leagues. Scouting is the heart of baseball.

Drayton McClane, Jr, Houston Astros former owner said, "Scouting is paramount in our organization. We have forty-two full time scouts who focus in on 2,000 players a year. They then bring down the number from 800 to 400. After much cross-checking, the players are scrutinized by the district scouter. Then a handful of the very best are measured by top management, during which time, there is a psychological profile test and a good look at the player's home life. Every prospect is thoroughly checked out."

P.S.: In 2002 when the new stadium was built several beer companies wanted their brand to be named on the stadium. McClane known for his Christian background chose the beverage subsidy Minute Maid owned by the Coca Cola company. A contract of 100 million over 30 years. Some now call it, "the Juice Box."

Bert Wells, the Dodger scout who signed Fred and me, said, "There is a certain make-up that is needed to be a pro and most observers call it, 'God given'." I always felt grateful to have had that God given baseball ability. I knew it still took hardwork.

Our scout spent four years watching our games to be sure we were prospects worth the investment. The first and only meeting with Mr. Wells, was the afternoon we signed our contracts. I was surprised at how much he knew about us. He was aware of Fred's winning hit and my pitching to lead our Wichita High School North team to the Kansas Championship. He even traveled to Hobart, Oklahoma where we played semipro ball in the Red River Valley League. In 1953, reports were sent to him about our play in Valentine, Nebraska in the Basin League. During two years at the University of Oklahoma, he personally followed us closely and had several conversations with Coach Jack Baer. What blew my mind, was his awareness, we regularly attended Wellington Place Baptist church. Our personal lives were important in his scouting decisions.

Actually, it was Dodger pitcher, Carl Erskine, who had a subtle influence upon me to sign with the Brooklyn organization. He was known as a pitcher who had a heart for God. It wasn't that he was planning to be a preacher or anything like that, but he lived a good life on and off the field. I liked the thought of being on the same team with him. In March of 2010, Erskine received Indiana's Sachem Award, the highest honor for lifetime excellence, moral virtue and community involvement. Erskine was quoted in the *Indianapolis Star,* "When I come to something as significant as this, I go to my lock box and I get out one of my World Series rings, then looking back.

… you know what I think today? So what?" His attitude about his baseball feats is one of true humility.

Even the most alert and knowledgeable baseball men, do not always recognize talent in untried hopefuls. Five feet, six inch, Phil Rizzuto, worked out at Brooklyn's Ebbets Field and was brushed aside by Casey Stengel. Soon afterwards, Phil was discovered by Yankee scout Paul Krichell and went on to become one of the great shortstops of all time. Many other players, have similar stories to tell of turn-downs before being signed.

The aim of professional baseball scouting is to secure the ideal team. The name of the game is to win, not only now, but also in the future. That means having the very best players possible. Baseball historian, Hugh Poland, in his unique devotional book, *Steal Away,* shares the philosophy of the great pitcher Robin Roberts, when he was a manager, "My feeling is that when you're choosing players on your team, you have to pick the right ones and then pray a lot."

When Whitey Herzog managed the Kansas City Royals and later the St. Louis Cardinals, he developed a reputation for building a ball club without buying or trading players. Bill James, baseball historian and statistician wrote, "He believes in building a ball club out of ball players."

Likewise, Jesus built his church out of believers. Simon Peter said, "You are the Christ, the Son of the living God." Jesus responded, "Upon this rock I will build my church and the gates of hell will not overcome it." Jesus was going to build his church with believers who knew that he was the Son of God.

"As Jesus was walking beside the Sea of Galilee, he saw two brothers, Simon called Peter and his brother Andrew. They were casting a net into the lake, for they were fishermen. 'Come follow me,' Jesus said, 'and I will make you fishers of men.' At once they left their nets and followed him."

We think of the twelve disciples as old gray bearded men. How misinformed we have been. Perhaps our perception has been influenced by Leonardo Da Vinci's wonderful presentation of the Lord's Last Supper.

He painted it on the wall of the refectory of the Dominican convent of Santa Maria in Milan, Italy in 1496-98. His portrayal of the twelve with Jesus, gives the perception that most of them were older than Jesus.

An intriguing article in *Southwestern Baptist News*, by Southwestern Baptist Theological Seminary professor, Dr. Ben Thompson, indicates that these disciples were in their twenties or even younger. Peter, the oldest, was probably in his late twenties. Jesus was approximately thirty years old when he started his public ministry, but the Bible is virtually silent about the ages of the disciples.

Dr Thompson's study reveals, "Mixing together the knowledge of the Jewish *Mishnal* and *the Talmudim,* we get a clearer picture of the Disciples. The *Mishnal* indicates that twenty is the age of pursuing an apprenticeship and thirty, the age of authority. The *Talmudim* informs us that these learners are the ones who go beyond home schooling to community schools taught by rabbis. Many would travel around the country with their students." As Jesus walked throughout Palestine with his team of twelve it was in accord with the practice of the day. There were many such bands; one was led by John the Baptist. Often, people addressed Jesus as, "Rabbi" or "teacher," because he taught and ministered as he traveled.

Dr. Thompson further indicates, "When Jesus was in Capernaum, he instructed Peter to find a shekel coin in the mouth of a fish, which was sufficient to pay the Temple tax for Peter and himself. The other disciples were old enough to follow him, but they were not old enough to be required to pay the Temple tax." The Disciples were apprentices, in other words like rookies, following Jesus. The word disciple, means learner and that's what they were!

Many times, a baseball manager, standing in the entry of the dugout shakes his head and stares skyward after some bonehead rookie play. They are the pride of the future but they come with a bag of greenhorn mistakes and errors.

The most famous rookie mistake in baseball, has been dubbed the Merkleboner. In 1908, Fred Merkle of the New York Giants, made a huge mental error in one of the last games of the season that eventually cost his team the pennant. The bone head play is described thoroughly by Leonard Koppett in his, *Concise History of Major League Baseball.* "In the last game of the season between the New York Giants and the

Chicago Cubs, the score was tied 1 to 1 in the bottom half of the ninth inning. With two outs, the Giants had Moose McCornich on third and Fred Merkle, the rookie, who had just singled, on first. Al Birdwell then lined a clean hit to center. McCornich came home to score. Giants win 2 to 1, but wait a minute, not yet. The overflow crowd of 20,000 immediately poured onto the playing field. Merkle, who was halfway to second base, saw the crowd and instead of touching second base, took off for the center field club house. Evers, the Cubs second baseman called for the ball, but the Giants third base coach had retrieved the ball. The Cubs players converged on the Giant's coach to get the ball back, but he threw it far into the crowd. Somehow the Cubs produced a ball and tagged second.

The Cubs first baseman, Chance, urged the umpires, Hank O'Day and Bob Emslie to call Merkle out, nullifying the run. Surrounded by the crowd, both flustered umpires refused to issue a clear decision. It seemed to be a 2 to 1 Giant victory.

But that night Cub Manager filed his report with the League's president, who upheld the forced play as an out and called the game a 1 to 1 tie. The Merkleboner game was finished the next day, and won by the Cubs 4 to 2 to win the pennant. Merkle caused his team to lose the game because he didn't touch second base."

Rookie Fred Merkle was dubbed, "Bonehead Merkle" for the rest of his life. He was only a twenty-two year old rookie, when he gave baseball one of its most enduring legends. Merkle went on to play top Major League ball for more than fifteen years, but that play was all people remembered.

What did Jesus see in those twelve men he called to be his disciples? At first glance, some could have written them off as a bunch of losers. Jesus spent much time in prayer, before making his selections, because he knew how much depended on his choices. Even then, Judas Iscariot, became a traitor. This was no mistake; Jesus knew Judas would be instrumental in his death on the Cross. Jesus called an unusual assortment of guys to follow Him. None were rich or powerful. They were all young, working men: fishermen, farmers, and even a hated tax collector.

The disciples of Jesus were not an ideal religious group. Glancing at some of these unknowns, one would almost question the Lord's discernment. A rundown of the twelve quickly raises doubts as to why they were chosen. Take a look at this line up!

Peter - impulsive, offensively boastful, short-tempered and cowardly
James - ambitious, jealous, fiery, needed the strength of his brother, John
John - prejudiced, jealous, ambitious, inexperienced in life
Matthew - mercenary, crafty, disloyal countryman
Thomas - doubter, criticizer, little faith
Andrew - lived in the shadow of his brother, Peter
James - the son of Alphaeus, nothing else mentioned
Nathaniel - skeptical, also known as Bartholomew
Philip - slow learner
Simon - zealot, difficult to control
Thaddeus - only a trace of his his name is mentioned
Judas Iscariot – high regard for money, the one who betrayed Jesus

Regardless of their personalities, they were part and parcel of the chosen twelve.

In baseball terms these men were not seasoned veterans in any sense of the word. They were all new followers. Peter, James and John, who were of the "inner circle," were also inexperienced young men. Their spiritual shallowness caused our Lord concern and at times he needed to settle petty arguments among them. "Be of good cheer," were his words that lessened their fears and anxiety in the face of fierce opposition. Several times, he had to show them his kingdom was not of this world. Many times Jesus had to explain the meaning of his simple stories so they could understand. Those three years walking with Jesus, were true learning experiences for these "Rookies of the Faith." He chose them not for what they were, but knowing what they were to become!

Once, when Jesus was addressing a large crowd he said, "The words I have spoken to you are spirit and they are life." But that wasn't what the people wanted to hear. They wanted an earthly king, so they would not accept him and his words. Many began to leave. Then Jesus turned and offered the twelve an opportunity to disband by asking, "Will you also go away?" Peter stepped up to the plate and hit a spiritual home run. "To whom shall we go? You have the words of eternal life!"

Jesus knew the Cross was coming and he wanted to strengthen their faith, so they would keep on believing. He had called them to walk with Him all the way to the Cross and beyond. After Jesus arose from the grave, they finally got it!

Yet, Jesus had chosen them. He signed them up. They were starters in his line up. Look at the confidence Jesus had in those rag tag disciples whom he had called and entrusted. "Go and make disciples in all nations." Together, they teamed up to become the mightiest force in history, the church of the Lord Jesus Christ.

Some years ago, Pastor Buster Reeves of the Temple Baptist Church in Redlands, California, invited me to speak at a special banquet for his congregation. He advertised the meeting, "A former Dodger pitcher, now preacher, will speak." This got the interest of George Blackerby, an eighty- four year old former Chicago White Sox outfielder, who played in 1925. During that service, Blackerby came forward to commit himself to Christ. The old ball player was later baptized by Pastor Reeves along with six members of his family. He signed up for Jesus!

The Bible tells us about a man who had a similar experience. He was the chief jailer in the Philippian prison and in charge of the Apostle Paul and Silas, who were prisoners. Paul and Silas prayed and sang hymns that night, while the other prisoners listened. At midnight a strong earthquake almost destroyed the prison, shaking open all the doors and every prisoner's chains came loose. The jailer, supposing the prisoners had fled, was about to kill himself, but Paul cried out, "We are all here!" The jailer brought Paul and Silas out and said, "Sirs, what must I do to be saved?" And they said, "Believe in the Lord Jesus and you shall be saved, you and your household." After Paul spoke with him and his family, they were all baptized.

You too, can respond to Jesus' personal call, "Come and follow me," because you have been called and chosen!

Jesus calls us, o'er the tumult
Of our life's wild, restless sea,
Day by day His sweet voice soundeth,
Saying, "Christian, follow me."
Cecil Frances Alexander

The dugout is a team's bench located in foul territory between home plate either at first or third base. There are two dugouts, one for the home team and one for the visiting team. This is where players sit when not at bat or in the field. It is located a few feet below the playing field which allows spectators to see, specifically the home plate area of play.

The roof of the dugout gives a place of refuge for disappointed players to hide after an awful strike out, error or pitching performance. I remember my first loss in proball. I had won six in a row. But then the bottom fell out! Two home runs were hit in the first inning. I was devastated! When manger Jack Banta came to the mound to rescue me, I welcomed the safety of the dugout.

When the people would not listen to the prophet Jeremiah, in discouragement, he cried out, "Oh, that I had in the desert a lodging place for travelers, so that I might leave my people and go away from them." We believers have solace in scripture, "your life is now hidden with Christ in God."

For all of us who have struckout or gone 0 for 4 in life, we can by faith in Jesus rejoice with the Psalmist, "You are my hiding place, you will protect me from trouble and surround me with songs of deliverace!"

CHAPTER 5
THE DUGOUT GOSPEL

A Little Leaguer's Prayer

Lord, give me strength to hit that ball;
And if I should, don't let me fall.

Help me to pick the one that's right;
Then let me knock it 'way out of sight.

Then help me run, with deer-like grace;
Don't let me slip, but tag first base.

Then on to second, stay with me, Lord;
'Cause this one out we can't afford.

Then let me zoom like a flying bird,
Right down the line and on past third

Then let me slide, with foot out-thrust;
Across home plate, through swirling dust.

But first of all, dear Lord, I pray,
Just tell the coach to let me play.
Don J. Gates

NO ATHLETE OF any description wants to sit in the dugout when the game is in full swing. The fun is in playing the game, not sitting and watching. But every great athlete has had his turn on the bench. Hall of Famer, Sandy Koufax, the greatest pitcher of the 50s and 60s sat the bench in a Dodger uniform for nearly three years before his regular pitching days. Dodger Manager Walter Alston said of Sandy, "He wouldn't have been with us, but for the league ruling about bonus babies."

In 1955, a new bonus rule was adopted; if a player received $4,000 and above, he had to stay on the Major League active roster for two years or be put up for grabs. This prevented the possibility of the player being bought by another club. Sandy signed with the Dodgers for a $25,000 bonus in December of 1954, so he had to be on the big team roster, whether he pitched or not.

I signed with a $4,000 bonus in September of that year and spent my three years in the minors. But, a least, I was pitching every four or five days and compiled a 17 - 6 record my first year. Sandy rarely got to play and Alston further said, "Sandy only pitched when the game was hopelessly lost. Then, anybody would do and I mean just anybody!"

When I think of old time seasoned stars like Lou Gehrig and Mel Ott as teenagers sitting the bench in the dugout, it is mind boggling. You do not become a star sitting on the bench, but that's where a star usually begins his career.

When I played on my first baseball team at eleven, the name of the game was sitting the bench. Boy, did I want to play in a real game. Then one day it happened. Our coach, Mr. Leslie Davis, let me bat. Somehow, I managed to hit a grounder to short. The shortstop muffed it and the ball went between his legs into the outfield, so I was safe at first base on an error. My twin brother, Fred, was up next and hit a double, which landed me on third with Fred on second. I was as scared as a jack rabbit. My heart was pounding so loudly, I thought it would jump right out of me.

Fred, on second, was as jumpy as I, for it was his first time on base, too. Our coach at third base, seeing his two nervous rookies on the base paths, cupped his hands and hollered above the excitement, "Don't move unless I tell you and then, run!" His last words were lost in the noise of the small crowd as our next batter, Darryl Klassen, hit a long high fly to left field.

"Run, Run!" yelled our overexcited coach. Down the third base line I flew toward home plate. To the surprise of our coach, the little outfielder made an amazing catch of the fly ball. In the midst of the noise, Mr. Davis came running wildly toward me at home plate, screaming at the top of his lungs, "Go back to third!"

Confused and excited, I ducked my head and tore back to third base for all my worth. Just as I was sliding into third, Fred, was motoring around third and passed me up, heading for home. He slid into home plate ahead of the throw from the outfielder and thought he had won the game. But, the ump called both of us out because Fred had passed me up on third base.

It is rare in baseball for the batting side to cause an out, since the defense is in control of the ball 100% of the time. Therefore, when the defensive team is in the field of play it seems impossible for the offensive team to cause an out, let alone a double out, but we terrible twins did it that day. My brother and I were double-trouble! Our first game landed both of us back on the bench.

It's extremely unusual, but it happens in the majors too. According to *Uncle John's Reader*, "In 1976 Phillies catcher, Tim McCarver, came up to bat with the bases loaded. Not known for his power, McCarver hit a deep fly ball. He watched it as he ran toward first base and was elated when it sailed over the wall! McCarver put his head down and kept on running. One problem: Gary Maddox, the runner at first, held up to make sure the ball wasn't caught. McCarver ran right past him. By the time he realized his goof, it was too late. He was called out for passing a runner, thus negating his grand slam."

Life can be like that, too. Just when we think we have it all together, we find ourselves being called out. It happened to a man in the Bible. His name was John the Baptist. If he had been an athlete, he probably would have ended up in the Hall of Fame.

John the Baptist, was a powerful preacher and wore unusual camel hair clothing with a large leather belt. His preached, "Repent, for the kingdom of God is at hand." People from all around came to the Jordan River to hear him, confessing their sins and being baptized.

I suppose, he was the "Billy Graham" of his day. But far more than that, John the Baptist was the forerunner of Jesus Christ. He was the first one to point to Jesus and say, "Here is the Lamb of God who takes away the sin of the world." Infact he baptized Jesus in the Jordan River.

One day, John found himself on the sidelines in the religious world. King Herod had put him in prison. His preaching had become too personal for the king. In John the Baptist's blunt fashion, he had fearlessly, taken Herod to bat and accused him of committing adultery for stealing his brother's wife.

No longer was John by the riverside, preaching and baptizing. No longer were the crowds following him. No longer was he a religious star. He was on the "bench in the dugout", in prison. All alone, John the Baptist became discouraged and confused. Now, as the forgotten prophet, doubts began to creep into his mind. The truth, he was once so sure of, became a question, "Was Jesus really the Messiah?" He had to hear the truth once again or go mad in his now silent stadium.

So he sent messengers to Jesus to ask, "Are you the one, or do we expect someone else?" Jesus sent back the answer to John's friends, "Tell John what you are hearing and seeing: how the blind see, the lame walk, the lepers made clean, the deaf hear, the dead are raised to life and the Good News is preached to the poor. How happy is he who has no doubts about me!" John the Baptist no longer had to live with a question mark for now he could live with an exclamation point about his Savior!

Many times a manager will put a bench warmer in the line up, even though it may not be in the best interest of the club, at that time. He realizes, that if a player sits in the dugout too long, he may begin to doubt his ability to compete.

Johnny Bench, caught for the Cincinnati Reds for sixteen years and was selected fourteen times as an all-star and was inducted into the Hall of Fame in 1989. When hosting the television series, *The Baseball Bunch*, he related a high school baseball game in Benger, Oklahoma. "I was called off the bench to pinch hit when I was a junior. I hit a home run to win the game." The interviewer asked, "Did you get to start the next game?" Johnny, in his casual Oklahoma drawl, said "Naw, it was back to the bench, cause you didn't take the place of a senior in Benger." As a bench warmer, Johnny was ready. He wasn't just sitting the bench. He was watching and waiting for his chance.

In 1907, I. E. Sanborn, baseball manager, made an observation that has become a baseball truism. "The strength of a modern major league team lies in its substitutes." Yogi Berra, gave a good New York slang expression in 1973, when his relief pitchers were not getting results. "If you don't have a bullpen, you don't have nothin'!"

The bullpen is a designated place, usually under the stands or beyond the outfield. Here, relief pitchers limber up during a game to be ready when they are called upon to pitch. Some people think the bullpen is a place for "bull sessions" of nonsense by a bunch of pitchers and catchers. Where the term comes from is anybody's guess. Some claim the name came from early day baseball, when the warm up area for pitchers in New York was under a Bull Durham billboard. To me, it is the perfect picture of the Spanish bull fighting arena. When the trumpet is blown, the gate opens and out comes the snorting fierce bull!

A 2009 issue of *Sports Illustrated* states, "When the Yankee's great closer, Mariano Rivera, comes to the bullpen, he gets ready by sticking to his routine regardless of the emotional pressures of the game. He goes through it whether it's in the middle of the season or the World Series. He stretches his whole body in the seventh inning of a close game. Then, he loosens his shoulder in the eighth by making circles with his right arm while holding a weighted ball. After that, he begins warming up by throwing three tosses to the catcher, making sure the mechanics of his delivery feel just right. Then, he begins pitching in earnest. He knows there isn't time to do his needed routine when he is called in to pitch. The preparation must have already been completed." So, when the door of the bullpen swings open, he is ready for the moment. Out comes the fiercest closer of them all … Mariano Rivera!

The bullpen is like the dugout bench in many ways. It's not a place to idly look at the game. You've got to be alert and ready for action. Pitchers concentrate on hitters and the progress of the game. The long reliever is ready at the beginning innings for that early call from the manager, knowing he may be pitching throughout the entire game. The middle reliever is up and ready from the third or fourth inning. Then there is the call for a situation reliever, such as a lefty pitcher facing a lefty hitter. The set-up man is the eighth inning pitcher, who gives all he's got in that late inning. The closer is the "money man," who finishes the game.

I was a starting pitcher for the Reno, Nevada Dodgers farm team, The Silver Sox. As a minor league team, we were limited in the number of pitchers on the squad. Therefore, after a game that I pitched, the manager usually called on me to relieve two games later. So, in the dugout I studied each opposing team's hitters for tell-tale signs of weakness. I knew to be ready for an instant call from our manager, Ray "Little Buffalo" Perry. I was mobilized for action!

In North high school, I was privileged to pitch under flamboyant coach, A.R. "Monk" Edwards. During my junior year, I played first base, and felt I would play there my senior year. We had two good pitchers, but Charlie Russell graduated at midterm and Kenny Yoke had serious back surgery and could no longer play. Monk, had heard I pitched some in summer ball, so, in desperation, he asked me, "Frank, would you be willing to try out for the pitching position?" He took me to the side lines during practice and said, "Go ahead and see if you can hit the catcher's mitt." After two good throws he said, "That's enough, you're on the mound from here on out."

A sports reporter from the *Wichita Eagle* newspaper, came to our practice just before the season opened. "Say, "Monk", how is your pitching staff this year?" To the newsman's surprise, "Monk" retorted, "Lefty Frank Minton is my starter, he is my reliever and he is my closer." Actually, we had a good right hand pitcher, Rod Hartley.

I was the starting pitcher in most of our games. From the very first game, pitching was easy for me. I didn't have a fancy curve ball or stuff like that. I just reared back and threw the ball. That regular season I lost only two games. Both were against our cross-town rival, East High School. High school baseball games are seven innings, but in the second game I pitched 11 1/3 innings. Our shortstop made two errors in the bottom half of that inning causing us to lose (1-0).

Because I had pitched that long, extra inning game, the next day the Kansas High School Athletic Association changed the rules, stating, "No pitcher could pitch more than nine innings in any twenty-four hour period." With that new rule in place, our North High team went into the play-off series for the State Championship.

In the first game, I started against a western Kansas consolidated school from the Victoria area that we easily defeated in five innings by a lop-sided score, 15-0. I was the winning pitcher and struck out twelve batters. The next day, we won 8-0 against Wyandotte, a Kansas City high school, who was favored to win the championship. I continued to rear back and throw straight fast balls and struck out eleven of their hitters, giving up only one hit in the five inning game. This game was also shortened, because of the eight run rule, at the end of the fifth inning. This game ended at 9 p.m.

Because of the new twenty four-hour rule, I was not eligible to pitch until 9 p.m. the next evening in the championship game. When I came in to pitch against El Dorado, relieving Rod Hartley, it was the third inning, with the score 5-3, runners on second and third and two outs. The first batter I faced was their great hitting catcher, Bolin. He hit the first pitch and with a sharp single, tied the game, 5-5. From then on, I threw fast balls with all my strength and struck out ten of the next eleven batters.

In the top half of the last inning with two outs, our second baseman, Leon Magner, went to first on a walk. My twin brother, Fred, stepped up and knocked a booming triple against the outfield wall, scoring Magner. Then, Fred continued home on an overthrow to third base. The score was now 7-5, our favor. I went to the mound the last of the seventh inning, and struck out the remaining three batters including the best hitter in the league, catcher Bolin. Fortunately, I was the winning pitcher of all three tourney playoff games. It was the second time our Wichita High School North Redskins had won the Kansas High School Baseball Championship! There was joy in "Mudville!"

Wichita High School East, the Blue Aces, was our cross-town rival. Their colors were, of course, blue and white. Our North High Redskins colors were red and white. The Redskins is no longer the school's mascot. In 2011 the Wichita school board voted down its name to be replaced.

On East's campus there is a large sculpture of a Trapper and an Indian each holding muskets. One morning the statue appeared, with a small splash of red paint. Likewise, one Monday morning when we arrived at school, one of the sculptured Indian heads that decorated the corners had a splash of blue carved on the corners of our building. So, you can see the rivalry between the schools was pretty intense.

On that same championship high school team, we had a utility outfielder, whose position for two years was sitting the bench. That was the name of the game for Booth. He came to every practice and every game, but he never got a chance to play.

Now, Booth didn't look like a baseball player. He wore glasses with big black plastic rims and his proper English with clear diction made him seem a little out of place among the average baseballer. In fact, he was the chess champion of our school. Nonetheless, Booth practiced as hard as anyone. Even though he came to play, it was always the bench for him.

In the fifth inning of a game against East, the Blue Aces, the score stood 2-1 in their favor. We had Harold Dwyer on second and Wayne Wise on first. "Monk" began looking for a pinch-hitter. Pacing up and down in front of our bench, he spied Booth. "Do you think you can hit that pitcher?" A surprised Booth answered, "I'm ready!"

"Well then, grab a bat!" our coach replied. Booth quickly selected his bat, and in a few moments was standing at the plate ready to swing at anything in sight.

The first pitch came whistling toward the plate. Booth swung and to our happy surprise, hit a line shot between right and center field. It was a sure double and maybe more. By the time the center fielder could retrieve the ball, the two base runners had scored, and the amazing bench warmer had slid into third base with a triple. The score now read 3-2, North High's favor!

"Monk" Edwards called time out, dusted off his new-found clutch hitter and said, "Well, Booth, you had it in you and I wish I'd seen it sooner." During his two years on the bench, Booth was watching and ready to play. His opportunity came and he grabbed it! Booth became a starter and a letterman.

To my pleasant surprise my high school awarded me a place in their, "Hall of Fame." The trophy presented to me reads:

> Frank Minton
> Wichita North High School
> Hall of Fame
> Inducted 2018
> Politics, Humanitarium, sports.

Saturday, October 7th, 2017

REV. FRANK D. MINTON '52

Politics/Humanitarian

Frank's first week at North he met his wife of 65 years, Joyce, in the Tower entrance hallway. While attending North High he was elected Boys Vice President, was in National Honors Society, was active in Drama and was a baritone in the North High Singers. As a football and baseball letterman, he pitched the Redskin baseball team to win the '52 State Championship, winning all three tournament games. Frank received a full baseball scholarship from the University of Oklahoma, where he received his Bachelors in Business Administration. He signed a three year bonus contract as a left handed pitcher with the Brooklyn Dodgers Organization and turned down his fourth year contract to enter the Gospel Ministry. In 1958 Rev. Minton founded the Tyler Road Baptist Church in their new home "The Dell" in Wichita. Its ministry expanded to include the Believers Baptist Church in Northwest Wichita. Frank received two divinity degrees from Southwestern Seminary in Fort Worth, Texas and pastored 10 churches in 6 states. In 1968 Rev. Minton held baseball clinics throughout Venezuela. He served as trustee of Missouri Baptist University and has been president of several national religious organizations, being elected in 1973 as Vice President of the 35,000 memb SBC Pastor's Conference. He went on to author two books: <u>Baseball's Sermon on the Mound</u> and <u>Baseball Hits and Bible Bits</u> and continues to pastor in Sugar Land, Texas.

After our championship high school season, my brother and I considered baseball scholarship opportunities in College. We decided that our next step was college instead of a pro contract. There were three universities that we considered: Kansas, Oklahoma, and Oklahoma State. After visiting all three campuses, we chose The University of Oklahoma.

The Sooners' baseball coach, ex-pro ball player, Jack Baer, had been OU's coach for ten years. Under his coaching, the baseball teams were perennial leaders in the Big Seven Conference (now the Big 12). OU had surprised the college baseball world by winning the 1951 College World Series in Omaha. The team went undefeated throughout the tournament and beat favored Tennessee 3 - 2 in the finals. The determining factors for our choice were: the school's splendid baseball history, Coach Baer's professional baseball background and the team's CWS championship. We accepted the University of Oklahoma scholarships and in the fall of 1952 moved to the campus at Norman, Oklahoma.

At that time, the NCAA would not allow freshman athletes of any sport to play on the varsity level. This was a big disappointment and a real downer for me. I worked out as hard and long as the varsity guys and as far as I could tell my studies were not adversely affected. In fact, the next year as a varsity player, my grades improved. Out of the three hundred or so scholarship athletes in all sports at OU, I placed fifth in academic rating.

The only bright spot in my freshman year was when Joe Mobra and I teamed up to pitch and shut out the varsity in an inter-squad game 1-0. My twin, Fred, drove in the only run with a homer off of Mac Sanders. At that time, I was enrolled in the Geology school, later changing my major to Business. Yet, I knew God was still pressing me to acknowledge His call to preach.

My sophomore varsity year was lackluster for me and our team. We placed second in the league to the University of Missouri and missed our chance to go to the College World Series.

Both summers of my two college years were filled with OU semi-pro teams in Hobart, Oklahoma and Valentine, Nebraska. The competition was good, but still not enough to satisfy me. I was ready to become a pro. After two years on the campus, I signed a bonus contract with the Dodger organization. Still tucked away in my heart, was God's call to preach. So I promised, "God, if you will allow me to be a Dodger for a few seasons, I'll be your preacher."

God was good and gave me three of the happiest years of my life pitching in the Dodger organization. In the years 1955 - 57, I had a win-loss record of 39 wins and 20 losses. As much as I loved the game, I knew that God had a life plan of purpose beyond baseball for me. Even knowing that, it still was one of the hardest decisions of my life to leave the game. So at the age of twenty-three, I yielded to His calling with eagerness. Leaving baseball was, in a spiritual sense, leaving the dugout and getting into the game. It was like trading a baseball diamond for a Bible crown.

God's call, answered

My fourth year contract was sent by registered mails when Joyce and I were living in Wichita, Kansas in the off-season. It was an exciting moment!

Joyce and I sat at our dining room table and talked about the Dodger contract invitation. She was delighted remembering our honeymoon year in Reno and it was a good season for my pitching record of 14 wins and 8 losses. Our baseball future looked as bright as the promises of God.

Yet, the call of God was embedded in my heart, I felt it had become urgent! Joyce assured me as we discussed baseball and God's call, "If you want to be a baseball player, I'll go with you. If you want to be anything I'll go with you!" God had worked in her heart too!

It was said to me when I did not go to Spring Training, "Look Minton," old guys preach, young guys play baseball." But I became like the prophet of God, Isaiah, when he answered God's call," Then I heard the Lord saying, "Who will go?" and Isaiah said "Here am I, send me!"

It wasn't an easy decision. But I knew I resisted his call long enough. I knew the time had come to let the baseball bridges of return burn!

Like the susbtitle of my book it had been a struggle but there was joy in my heart for I was "trading a Diamond for a Crown!"

A Christian song that has always penetrated my heart:

> Must Jesus bear the Cross alone
> And all the world go free?
> No, there's a cross for everyone,
> And there's a cross for me.

The years have flown by and baseball is still with me. Where ever I preach I get rapt attention when I illustrate my sermons with a baseball story. The following Post Cards magazine article reveals that I am still "Dodger Blue" and "True Blue" to God's calling.

Mustard Seed Moments: Walking the Talk

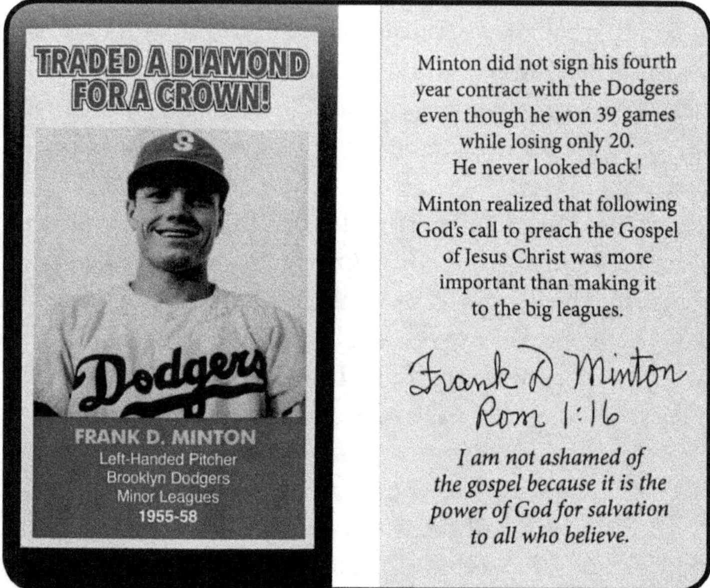

- With Frank Minton
minton.frank@gmail.com

Living in Walden on Lake Conroe for 15 years has been a pleasure, but for me, it has a distinct spiritual dimension. Several times a week, I walk the land barrier between the lake and the marina—my attempt to stay in shape, a routine from my Brooklyn (now Los Angeles) Dodger days. As I walk along, I hand out a business card (made to resemble a baseball card with a photo of me as a pitcher at age 20). On the back, it reads, "Minton realized that following God's call to preach was more important than making it to the Big Leagues."

I share a smile, briefly talk baseball, and tell them, "I never looked back!" I usually walk away, leaving it up to them if they want to converse further. The response has been amazing. Countless conversations and prayers have resulted. Broken hearts, divorce, loss of loved ones, confusion with life, and even thoughts of suicide have been openly confessed. One lady sitting lakeside asked, "Can I tell you my story? I'm mad at God!" Her husband had been killed in the war in Afghanistan. After pouring out her hurt, we prayed to God—twice!

So, for me, it's more than a walk to keep in shape. Sharing your faith as you go in everyday living is received better than you think. Give a pleasant hello and a winsome smile. Ask how they are doing. Start a conversation and listen! The Holy Spirit will lead you further (and you don't need a baseball card).

I can say with all sincerity, I have never looked back. I must admit though every March, I get that little urge called "spring training" and glance over my shoulder to see what my Dodgers are up to.

> "Brethern… this one thing I do, forgetting those things which are behind and reaching for those things that are before, I press toward the mark for the prize of the high calling of God in Christ Jesus." Me too Paul, I press on!

My first pastorate after pro ball was in the small Southwest Kansas town of Cunningham, which was surrounded by wheat fields. It was an hour's drive west of Wichita on the old "Cannon Ball," US highway 54. Cunningham was a typical farm and ranch community with wheat storage facilities and the proverbial, lone yellow flashing light for the highway traffic. The key building was the two story high school on Fourth Street, where the street ended and the wheat fields began..

There were three churches in Cunningham: Christian, Methodist and Roman Catholic, which had been part of the community since the 1880's. Each denomination had a small but adequate church-like building. In the late 1940's, an upstart group of Southern Baptist folks established a fledgling congregation, which met in a former auto mechanic's building. The congregation had built a steeple and cleared several lots around the church for a nice lawn and parking. Yet, this was a severe handicap, for it was not a churchy looking place to worship. It was the spring of 1958 when I became the rookie preacher in town. The town gossip was: "How could this young preacher have a window air-conditioner and wall-to-wall carpet in the living room of the church parsonage?" (items Joyce and I personally furnished)

A man knocked on the door and asked my wife about the furnishings. I smiled at her answer, "because he hasn't always been a preacher."

When news got out around town, the new Baptist preacher had just "retired" from pitching for the Dodgers, they were more accepting. (The distinction between a minor leaguer and a major leaguer was somewhat blurred) To my surprise, the small community of 415 people had a town team called The Cunningham Churchmen. They weren't a Christian bunch of players, to say the least, but they wore that name on their uniforms.

For years, the team had tried to qualify to play in the Kansas Semi-Pro Baseball Tournament at the Dumont-Lawrence stadium in Wichita, but it was never achieved. A few weeks after my arrival, the mayor came to visit and invited me to pitch for the team. He pleaded, "We especially need a good pitcher in a bad way."

There was just one catch. Since most of their players were farm hands, they could only play on Sunday. Well, that gave me a problem, because Baptists of that day had two worship services, one in the morning and a second, in the evening. So I declined the invitation.

This word got around to a few businessmen. The town banker called and asked if I would consider pitching during the week, if lights were installed on the field. I readily agreed to his offer. Within two weeks, the construction of lights on telephone poles was completed.

Our first game was on a Tuesday night and the farmers and townspeople came out of the wheatfields. Our opponents were from the larger town to the east, Kingman. The old wooden stands could only hold about fifty fans, so people drove their cars up to the sidelines as if it were a drive-in movie. While watching the game, they honked their horns when something exciting was happening. As I pitched, it took me a few innings to get used to these sounds.

It was not only a big night for the fans, but also for me. I must tell you, my heart was pumping with adrenaline, like you wouldn't believe.

Here I was, after playing three years of pro ball, feeling like I was in a little World Series. I just couldn't fail. I prayed as I pitched. "Lord, please let me do my best."

Those new, rather dim lights, were in my favor. You can imagine how difficult it was for batters to see my fast ball. Well, to make a good story even better, not only did we win, but I pitched a no-run, no-hit game! In my three years of proball I pitched a one hitter and a two hitter but never a no hitter.

The Cunningham Courier, has a by-line, "The only newspaper in the world that cares about Cunningham, Kansas." It ran a front page article stating "Cunningham Churchmen have come up with a winner!"

It was a great summer of church and baseball. In both arenas we prospered. Our church doubled in attendance from twenty to forty. During this time I was ordained to the Gospel Ministry by our little church. My college Pastor, Dr. E. F. Hallock brought the "charge" message and administered the "Laying on of hands" a Biblical tradition to publicly proclaim my ordination by vote of the Church.

Our baseball team qualified to go to the long anticipated tournament in Wichita. We won two and lost two games and were eliminated, but we received a hero's welcome by the folks in Cunningham. My ministry in Cunningham was a hit! It came to a close in the fall as I made plans to move back to Wichita and go to Midwestern seminary in Kansas City.

Before my Cunningham pastorate God had placed a "Field of dreams" in my heart, I knew as I pitched for the Dodgers that God was calling me to preach His Word, but where was yet to be revealed.

Even though having a fine house in our home town Wichita, Kansas, the "Field of dreams" for us was yet to be found. So Joyce and I began a search to find a place for a new home.

We found a large lot with a 240 foot frontage in a subdivision called "The Dell." We felt God's calling and assurance, "If you buy it a church will be born." It was a pie shaped lot on a curve some distance from any neighbor's homes on either side. We did not want to cause a problem with a beginning church group meeting in our home.

The architect worked on plans that called for a tri-level house which would fit nicely for worship in the half basement area with large windows on two sides.

The bedrooms in the second upper level housed the nursery, preschool and Children. The first level had the youth in the dining room with the adults meeting in the living area. My study was a guest bedroom next to the worship area.

On the very first Sunday, September 7, 1958 part of our "Field of Dreams" became a reality! Our first worship service was held in the lower level of our tri-level home with seventeen people present which included our two small children Bruce and Lori. It was awesome! The thrill reminded me of my first game I pitched for the Dodgers.

Working together has always been a baseball axiom. Church work is the same. Jesus sent disciples out to witness in His name, "two by two."

Pleasantview Church of Derby, Kansas, (located about 15 miles from our home) loaned us three wonderful families. The key family was the Larry Bell family of four with their teen daughter, Shirley who was our pianist. When she would learn a new song we gladly sang it in the Worship service.

We accomodated the church in our home for 15 months. It was a blessing!

An Email sent to us a few months ago by our first secretary who worked only on Saturdays.

> I always admired you, Joyce. On Sunday mornings you had your young children up, fed, dressed, beds made, house in order, early in time for People to arrive and go into every room of your home. Then back on Sunday evening and Wednesday. Then I was there on Saturday preparing the Sunday bulletin introuding into your home. You both gave a deeper meaning to the inscription on your fireplace: "As for me and my house we will serve the Lord."
>
> Thanks for the example.
>
> God bless, Twylah Hatcliff Young.

After I read Twylah's letter, It caused me to reflect upon a true moment as newly weds with our "Field of Dreams" church in our home.

The Children's area was directly above the worship place in the trilevel. This usually worked very smoothly.

One Sunday during worship as the small congregation was singing loud noises filtered down from the children's area. I immediately went up the two short stair ways and found my sweet wife with her hands full with seven children.

"Honey, what's going on? Can't you keep it down?" I blurted out to her. My usually "cool, calm and collected," bride said in a quite voice, "Frank, step out into the hall way", as she closed the door behind her. Suddenly, with out warning, she slapped me in the face and said with tears, "I am doing the best I can."

Ashamedly, I knew I had pushed my Joyce to her breaking point! Wow, what a wake up call from my little Sweet "Field of Dreams" companion. It was a slap that has lasted a life time! Today, "We are still in it together!"

I was so wrapped up in my calling and pastoral ministry it never occurred to me as to what my twenty three year old Joyce was willing to do to serve the Lord. I am grateful she shared in my "Field of Dreams."

My "Field of Dreams" Joyce and me in our "honey moon" year during my last year with the Dodgers.

Complicating our lives, I traveled to Kansas City to attend Midwestern Baptist Seminary four days a week. I would leave late on

Mondays with three other pastors and come home on Friday. It was an ordeal to say the least. But it was worth it!

Two incidents are worthy to note. As we traveled, we talked about the small churches we were pastoring. I was so excited about my "Field of Dreams", the church in my home and my true calling leaving the Dodger world, the guys would often say "OK Minton, that's enough!

On one of our travels, as I was driving my Volkswagon, I heard paper being torn up coming from the back seat. Suddenly, Calvin Miller burst out in tears, crying.

"What's going on, Calvin?" I openly asked. Calvin's response humbled all of us.

"I have been criticizing the Bible and writing it down, but your excitement about your work in the Lord touched my heart and I have repented!"

Dr. Calvin Miller became a distinguished college professor, acclaimed pencil drawing artist and author of fifteen interesting books that range from novel fiction to deep theology. His "Once upon a tree" became a best seller.

Another preacher passenger was in his first pastorate and real rookie. He made a number of errors and finally resigned his church. On the way home he asked our driver Jon Lurtz, to stop the car as we drove on the highway near his church field.

On the side of the highway he cupped his hands around his mouth and yelled as loud as he could, "Yepee !" Free, free at Last!" With that he got back into the car with a big smile on his face. Interesting, I never heard whether he continued in the ministry. I'll see him in heaven! At least he tried.

An interesting conversation is worth mentioning during the construction of our house after I had "retired" from baseball. We planned for a large Silvedale stone wood-burning fireplace to be built in our living room. It could be seen when entering the foyer. We planned to have an inscription in the cornerstone, which would read

The contractor suggested to me. "Son, (I was 23) "It may not be prudent to place such an, in your face, statement in stone. When you sale this home someday, it may keep a prospective buyer away." Joyce said that I responded with baseball candor. "Well, if they don't like it, they can just chisel it out, because its going in." To this day after more than sixty years, that cornerstone still sends out the Bible message.

Within a year, our small congregation had grown to more than 70 members. Then we found it, our "field of Dreams"! An entire city block of 5 acres on Tyler Road the major artery to Highway 54 was opened to us. The price of $17,000 was brought down to $13,000, a deal! Through prayer and searching by faith, Tyler Road Baptist Church had the "Field of Dreams" in which to build.

Today a large edifice welcome's, "Whosoever will may come." I smile with joy in my heart as a former Dodgers baseballer who heard the call, "If you build it a Church will be born!" Forgive me for placing God's calling to me in words for the movie, Field of Dreams."

The change from the pitcher's mound to the pastor's pulpit was dramatic. The experiences I had as a pitcher on the mound gave me confidence to preach in the pulpit. Some church members claimed that even my strides to the pulpit were similar to a pitcher's stride to the mound. In fact, one of my preaching professors, upon seeing my colorful sports jacket asked, "Is that what you wear in the pulpit, when you preach?" *Broadman Publishers*, printed their observation of my baseball swagger, "Frank D Minton is not what many people think as being "preacherly." I always liked that image!

During the rebellious sixties when I was pastoring the large south cliff Baptist Church in FortWorth, Texas several of our youth cut slits in the backlegs of my baptism waders. I baptized at the beginning of most worship services so I slipped the waders over my suit pants. After baptizing several I could feel the warm water. My pants were super wet!

When I walked to the platform and was about ten or twelve feet from the pulpit I tossed my Bible upon it. Wham! That of course got the attention of a thousand eyes. I pitched a fast ball sermon! After the service one of my deacons said I whispered to my wife, "This is going to be good!"

Some years later one of the guys apologized. Thinking about the event makes me smile.

Throughout my pastoral ministry, baseball was still an energizing force in my life. When I faced tough challenges as a pastor, I leaned back and remembered how I faced those batters when the bases were loaded. During those moments, I quietly prayed on the mound and I continued to pray the same way as a pastor. For me, baseball and the ministry have the same trust in the Lord.

In 1972, I was Senior Pastor of Tower Grove Baptist Church in St. Louis, the largest Baptist church in Missouri. There were a number of teens living near our inner-city church, who were involved in groups that you might call gangs. They were young and still not hardened.

Bob was the leader of a group of boys and girls from eleven to eighteen. They didn't have the money to wear black leather jackets, so in the summer their identification was white t-shirts and jeans. In the winter they wore inexpensive coats. Gray or black athletic shoes were their "running" attire. It was a real challenge to get them to come to our church, even though we had one of the finest youth athletic complexes in the nation.

Late one night, I received a call from the police. They were getting ready to arrest about seven of these kids. They had broken into our education building and were running around the fourth floor throwing Bibles and song books. The gang appealed to the police, saying they were church members and therefore, had a right to be in the building, even though it was 11pm.

When I arrived at the church, two police squad cars had their spot lights aimed at the kids, who were leaning with their hands pressed on the building. "Pastor, are these yours?" asked the sergeant. I admitted that I knew them and said, "I'll see that they'll go home, if you don't book them."

"O.K. pastor; you've got 'em." With those parting words, the police got into their squad cars; leaving me with my seven delinquents.

Confronting the leader, I said, "All right Bob, what's the story?" Before another word was said, Bob snapped his fingers with both hands and commanded, "Scatter!" Immediately, all the kids took off running in every direction, disappearing into the darkness.

Bob turned to me and almost yelled, "What's the deal Preach? You say 'Come to church, come to church' and then what do you do? You call the cops on us!"

I bounced back, "Come on, Bob, what's your deal? Eleven at night! You've got'ta be kidding!"

With that, Bob took off running across our dimly lit parking lot, heading for the streets. Well, I wasn't going to take that as the end of our conversation. Even though it had been fifteen years since my Dodger days, I was still in pretty good shape and I was going to catch up with that sixteen year old runaway, even if it was the last thing I did!

So, into the darkness we ran. Trailing him was not easy, but I caught glimpses of him as he ran down the alleys and across busy streets. Let me tell you, I was dodging car after car with horns blaring, but I was gaining on him and he knew it. Finally, Bob hollered over his shoulder, "Hey, Preach, I'll quit, if you will!"

With that I slowed down, and when Bob stopped, his back was toward me. I reached for his shoulder, turned him around and received one of the biggest surprises of my life! Bob buried his head in my chest and with tears cried out, "Oh, Preach, I wish someone would love me, just plain love me." (Even as I write this account there are tears in my eyes because of that heartfelt moment).

"Say, Bob, let's go get a 'Big Mac'." So off we went, preacher and gang leader. After a year or more of working with this group in our Sunday School, special youth meetings and recreation activities, Bob and a few of his gang came to know Christ as their Savior. What a privilege it was to baptize this street kid!

I remember my surprise when Bob came to my study one Friday and announced "If you want 'em you've got em." I lined them up and said, "Everybody on deck. We are going together!" I said, "Now Bob you know its an individual matter." All eleven Gang members came forward at the alter call.

Why did I chase Bob through those St. Louis Streets? Not to win an argument nor to show my prowess but because God had placed in my heart what Jesus said, "Love one another as I have loved you" and "as you go, make disciples."

It was from the baseball world, some fifteen years before, where I learned, "You have to get off the bench if you're going to play in the game." Hey preach, get out of your dugout in your study and go out into the streets after the lost! It will move your heart and make your sermons come alive!

Just before Jesus went to the Cross, he walked with his disciples to a place called Gethsemane, to pray through the night. He said "My soul is overwhelmed with sorrow to the point of death. Stay here and keep watch with me." Going a little further, he fell on his face and prayed, "My Father, if it is possible, may this cup be taken from me. Yet, not as I will, but as you will."

When Jesus returned; he found them sleeping. Again he said, "Watch and pray." He went away a second and third time to pray and each time when he returned they were asleep. On both disappointing returns he admonished them, "Watch and pray!" Jesus was telling his disciples, "Be alert; the time is at hand. Be ready!"

Bottom of the Ninth Haiku

The bases loaded-
Two outs and three runs behind:
No one to pinch-hit
R. Gerr

Abraham Lincoln said, "I shall wait and prepare and perhaps my time shall come." Your opportunity in life will come your way, perhaps in a time you least expect, yes, in a moment when you think not!

Must Jesus bear the cross alone
And all the world go free?
No, there's a cross for ev'ryone,
And there's a cross for me.
Thomas Shepherd

CHAPTER 6

A TIME FOR EVERY SEASON

There is a time for
everything,
and a season for every
activity under heaven …
Ecclesiastes 3:1

THE BEGINNING OF spring training brings the big announcement, winter is over and baseball has begun. I was thrilled to know every contracted ball player in the Dodger system received a free trip to spring training with all expenses paid. But of course, none of us were paid either. Our salaries began when the actual league games started.

From late February, through the beginning of April, fifteen major league teams play in Florida's Grapefruit League; the other fifteen teams compete in the Cactus League in Arizona. For the major leaguer in his prime, secure in his position on the team, it's a leisurely time: drills in the morning, golf in the afternoon, a gradual warm up for the long season ahead.

But, for a hopeful rookie like me, it was a time to catch on with the big club or for that matter any club. Spring training was a time of high anxiety, for there were impressions to be made and positions to be won. I learned the procedure to release a ball player came by way of a message to report to Dick Walsh's office. He was the Director of Minor Leagues and had this unpleasant task. I was always grateful I didn't get a message.

I was excited and nervous making my first flight from Kansas to spring training in Florida. It was a big deal even for a college guy. I remembered a Bible verse that I learned at the Baptist Student Center while attending Oklahoma University, "Trust in the Lord with all your heart and lean not unto your own understanding, but in all your ways acknowledge Him and He will direct your paths." That Bible bit was enough to ease my anxieties.

When I arrived at the Vero Beach airport, the shuttle van picked up my twin and me. We passed a Presbyterian church marquee that read, "Fear not tomorrow for God is already there." That gave me a wonderful confirmation for spring training.

Upon arriving, I was awed by the sight of hundreds of baseball players milling around the camp. Dodgertown was once a Navy training base during World War II. In 1955 those barracks were still in good condition. At that time, the major leaguers had their own separate barracks and each player had his individual room. We minor leaguers shared our quarters with as many as six in larger dorm rooms. Bunk beds were the norm.

The layout of the baseball fields was terrific. Eight or more diamonds were spread out all over the campus with Holman stadium being the centerpiece. I found that all teams from class D to the Majors worked out on these ball fields.

What struck me most were the palm and orange trees growing all over the place. Leaving cold Kansas in the morning and arriving that afternoon in this floral, balmy setting was surreal. I can still smell those sweet orange blossoms.

To my delight, the Dodger owner, Walter O'Malley, had large barrels filled with orange juice at every diamond. All a player had to do was turn on a spigot and the ice cold juice flowed. I just couldn't drink enough of it. I drank so much, after a few weeks, sores erupted on my right arm and I had to go to the camp clinic to get some medication. I wasn't the first player victimized by an orange juice overdose.

In 1942, Branch Rickey was hired by the Dodgers as general manager. He then created the spring training complex in Vero Beach, Florida. It was built into the finest baseball training facility in the world.

We were issued uniforms of the club we were assigned to in our contract. My team was the Ashville, North Carolina, class B league. The uniform had a large orange number on the back of the shirt. I was known by number instead of name. Somewhat humiliating compared to what I had in mind.

The Dodgers had a drag-net out for left-handed pitchers, when I signed. Therefore, the scouts concentrated on finding promising pitchers. Being one of those desired pitchers, I imagined I would probably receive some special attention from management. But, I found out in a hurry, my bonus contract didn't mean a thing. With more than 350 of us trying out for 168 positions, I realized there were no guarantees. A few days ago, I reminded Carl Erskine of this; he laughed and said, "I remember, 200 of you showed up, along with Sandy Koufax!"

Players usually stayed with their assigned teams the first few weeks, but as training days went on into late March and early April, there were big changes. Players were either cut from the roster and sent packing or moved to other teams. Going home without a team was a sad day for even the toughest guy. The hardest part of being released is facing the folks back home, who won't understand the competition and what a long hard endurance test it is to be a pro ball player.

To me, Dodgertown was a secular baseball shrine. Here, is where I trained for three years every spring for six weeks and loved every day of it. Joyce and I visited just as the news broke it was sold. Before the gates were closed we walked where I once played. Memories flowed of those past days in the Florida sun. As we walked, it once again became my "Field of Dreams;" I imagined Sandy Koufax, Roy Campanella, Jackie Robinson, Carl Erskine and Dodger manager, Walter Alston being here.

It reminded me, also, of the little Rose Park mission where I preached one of my first sermons. After a Wednesday evening Bible study, Pastor Rogers, of the First Baptist Church announced someone was needed to preach at the Rose Park mission this Sunday. My twin Fred said, "Hey Frank, here is your chance. You preach and I'll lead the singing." We enthusiastically approached pastor Rogers with our plan. "Well, if you think you can handle it," was his reluctant answer.

By Sunday, we recruited Don Demeter to be our lone usher and take up the offering. So, the three of us from Dodgertown took charge of the mission service. The little place was actually a large tent with a dirt floor. The mission was about one-third filled with forty in the congregation with a dozen kids. Fred, led the music, singing some good old Gospel hymns. True to his word, Don took up the offering, just before I went to the little home-made wooden pulpit to preach.

I preached from the Bible, using notes I had scribbled on some Dodger stationery. My sermon was entitled, "Those Dusty Roads of Life." I talked about Jesus' walk to the Cross, Jesus appearing to two disciples on the Emmaus Road after His resurrection, Paul's conversion on the Damascus Road and finally, Jesus saying, "I am the Way."

Afterward, several kids gathered around for autographs and wanted to know if we would be back next Sunday. We had committed to three weeks. So when we said yes, they cheered and promised to bring all their friends in the neighborhood. In those three weeks our little mission grew to a congregation of over one hundred, loaded with kids. It is still a precious memory of Dodgertown. The Forest Park mission is now a strong church in a beautiful edifice.

Former, great Dodger pitcher, Carl Erskine, describes Dodgertown in detail in his classic book, *Tales from the Dodger Dugout,* "Dodgertown was like a baseball college with hundreds of players throwing, hitting, playing intra squad games, and doing baseball drills. At night, after the evening meal, Mr. Ricky would assemble his many scouts and minor league managers in a large room, where the walls were lined with blackboards. Each board had one of the minor league team names written across the top. The purpose of the meeting was to select who could best fit teams from class D to class triple A. It was a competitive session for the managers present, all of whom wanted the best players they could get. Mr. Rickey would read a name, give some stats, and then discussion would follow. Each manager was eager to talk about why a particular good player was right for his team."

It's good to note that Rickey was not only a brilliant baseball executive, but also an experienced ball player. In 1906, as a rookie catcher, he was the first player from the St. Louis Browns to hit two dingers in one game.

Mr. Ricky was no longer the top executive when I came to camp; yet, the same procedures were still in place with Buzzie Bavasi in charge. The scouts and managers would be out on the fields every day with clip boards, jotting down notes about our play. It was impossible for them to know all the players in the system, because twenty or more teams were in spring training. Each team had numbers of a specific color for identification purposes. Notes such as, "orange 12 made a great catch and purple 7 threw a wild pitch," were written down.

The Dodgers new treasure, lefty pitcher Sandy Koufax, was also experiencing his first spring training. Even though a phenom, he was the wildest, fastest and greatest rookie pitcher of us all. I actually saw him throw a pitch over a practice diamond's backstop. Walter Alston, in his second year of the twenty-three he managed for the Dodgers, admitted he thought to himself, when he first saw Sandy pitch, "What do we have here?" Well, to the delight of Alston and the Dodgers, Sandy became the most spectacular left-handed pitcher in history! In 1968 Sandy struck out 382 batters! He attended the recent 2020 World Series which the Dodgers won!

We had a small medical clinic at Dodgertown. Perhaps, I had some of that preacher within me, so I would make a routine tour to see the baseball patients. One morning I was surprised to see Sandy in the infirmary with a mild case of mumps. Not knowing that he was Jewish, I offered a prayer, closing in the name of Jesus. He was good natured about it, so the next time I ventured in to see him, he said, "Go ahead Minton and lay a little Jesus on me." It was great to see Sandy on TV in the stands watching the Dodgers- Astros game during the 2017 World Series.

Workout sessions daily, one at 9 am and the other at 2 pm were normal routine. Our breakfast and lunch meals were ample, but not overdone. In fact, lunch usually consisted of a sandwich, soup and salad. We ate lunch in our uniforms. Our afternoon schedule prohibited a large, leisurely lunch. After the second workout, we showered and were ready for that delicious dinner. The cafeteria was a sensation. They served tasty evening meals and lots of it. Our favorite was the Saturday evening meal, which consisted of rib eye and T-bone steaks! Extra special meals were provided when a visiting Grapefruit League team would come to Dodgertown.

There was a large lounge area between several of the barracks, which was a great mixing place for the players. Every evening we would congregate to shoot pool, play cards and listen to piano and guitar music by the players themselves. There were a lot of bull sessions and laughter. Poker, drinking, gambling and smoking were prohibited. Some guys walked to town and went to a movie. Lights were out at 11 o'clock.

Sunday mornings there were no work-out sessions, so we had the opportunity to go to church. The Dodgers furnished bus transportation for the few church goers. We had several African-Americans in camp and my twin and I made friends with them. Being a Kansan, I never thought about the color line that existed in the south, during the middle fifties. One Sunday, we asked our black buddies to attend church with us. They were very reluctant, but finally relented. Boy, were we in for a shock when we tried to enter that Florida church. Immediately, three ushers closed rank and barred the door. Our black friends were gracious and quickly withdrew from the steps of the church. I was crushed! I always believed in the Bible teaching, "Whosoever will, may come."

Well, you can image my terrible dilemma. Safely back at Dodgertown, I had a lot to reflect upon. It made me appreciate these ball players' struggle for acceptance that I took for granted. What was so difficult for me to grasp, was that pro ball was nine years ahead of local churches in welcoming people of all races. Jackie Robinson became a Dodger in 1947; here it was 1955 and here were already dozens of black ball players in the Majors. I just shook my head in Christian shame!

That church experience made a lasting impression on me. As a pastor, I was determined to lead every church to an open door policy. Amen! The Bible gives evidence that all people were accepted. "Some of the Jews were persuaded and joined Paul and Silas as did a large number of God-fearing Greeks."

One Wednesday evening during spring training, Fred and I walked to a church prayer and Bible study service. The camp was almost one mile out of town and none of the ball players had cars. On our way back to

Dodgertown, a 1952 green pick up Ford truck stopped next to us. The driver rolled down the window and said, "Hey guys, hop in, I'm on my way to camp." We gladly jumped into the front seat with our Good Samaritan. "You must be the Minton twins," he continued. With those words, we knew we had the good fortune of being picked up by the Dodger manager himself, Walt "Smokey" Alston. As we rode to camp on what is now named Tommy Lasorda Lane, Alston asked, "Where have you guys been?"

"At church prayer meeting" we answered almost in unison. His response was a blessing to us, "I've been trying to call my wife all evening and couldn't figure out where she was. I should have known she was at church." That drive to camp showed us the heart of our famous manager, who soon thereafter became a baseball legend. It is amazing that Alston managed the Dodgers for twenty-three years with twenty-three one year contracts!

Walt Alston was a quiet, private person, with a soft voice and it was rare for anyone to receive praise from him. When the publisher wanted Alston's endorsement for my first book, *Baseball's Sermon on the Mound,* I felt it would be a futile attempt. The Dodgers public relations people said, "Mr. Alston does not give his name out for any endorsements." To my pleasant surprise, though, he gave these words to print, "**Frank D. Minton is a former member of the Dodger organization who has combined his baseball experiences and position as a pastor to produce an inspirational book. We think you will enjoy his efforts in his publication.**" I have to believe that short pick-up truck ride for two church guys had a lot to do with his recommendation. Before Alston became a Hall of Fame manager, he was a respected school teacher in Oxford, Ohio and a successful minor league manager.

As I pitched in this brand-new baseball world, my mind was flooded with deep thoughts of the future. The Christmas hymn, "O Little Town of Bethlehem," has words that were embedded in my heart. "The hopes and fears of all the years, are met in Thee tonight." The words, "Hopes and Fears," precisely described my anxiety.

Oh little town of Bethlehem
How still we see thee the lie,
above thy deep and dreamless sleep,
the silent stars go by
yet in the dark street shinning
the everlasting light,
The hopes and fears of the years,
Are met in thee tonight
Phillips Brooke 1835

These words gave me an inner peace that I could trust Jesus through it all.

Through it all, through it all,
I've learned to trust in Jesus,
I've learned to trust in God.
Though it all, through it all,
I've learned to depend upon His Word.
Andre Crouch

CHAPTER 7

AT THE BOTTOM OF THE TOTEM POLE

Analysis of Baseball

It's about
The ball,
The bat,
The mitt,
May Swenson

I F ANYONE COULD write something about the minor leagues of baseball, it would be me, because that's where I played my pro ball. The minors have changed considerably; the paychecks, transportation, lodging and the ball parks are all updated and improved. So, much of my expertise is from personal experiences years ago, but none-the-less, it's about the game we all love.

Covid19 gave minor league baseball almost a fatal blow in 2020 when the entire season was canceled! But this year fans in minor league cities are finally getting baseball back.

Brooklyn Cyclones manager Ed Blankmeyer said, "Small town baseball is in the fabric of the United States, its our culture." To see pro players in person once again gives pride along with family-friendly prices, off beat give aways and local yokel names makes baseball come alive with a sense of belonging.

Today there are fewer teams and leagues. What remains are four levels- triple A, Double A, high A and low A, each with regional names. This means 42 clubs have lost their connection to pro ranks.

The minors today will be testing ground for several rules and changes MLB is considering: automatic ball-strike system, restrictions on pitchers and infield positions for defensive plays also larger bases for safety. Best of all players salaries increased!

The minors taught me an attitude that has underlined my entire life. I learned from my experiences pitching on the mound, "It's not perfection I'm after, but the best performance I can command." I knew how good I could pitch and I also knew how bad. Like the Apostle Paul, "For I do not do the good that I want to do, but I practice the evil that I do not want to do. . . What a wretched man I am! . . Who will rescue me? … I thank God through Jesus Christ our Lord."

The cartoon, The Born Louser" by Art Sampson depicts an older man talking to a young baseballer. "How's your pitching coming along?"

"Not so good, everything is backwards! My fast ball is slow, my sinker rises and my curve doesn't"

Frank Bettger's award winning book, *How I Raised Myself from Failure to Success in Selling,* gives a graphic account of what he learned while playing minor league baseball. In 1907, he was playing third base for Johnstown, Pennsylvania, in the Tri-State League for $175 a month. To cover up his nervousness, he acted laid-back, with a nonchalant attitude. He was stunned, when his manager fired him. He asked him why and the manager said, "You played like you were tired and worn out." From then on, Frank was determined to play enthusiastically and never again have anyone think he was lazy.

He finally caught on with a team at the bottom of the totem pole, in Chester, Pennsylvania of the Atlantic League for $25 a month. After ten days, because of his hustle and enthusiasm, he began playing for a New Haven, Connecticut team and his salary was increased to $185 a month. He continued his enthusiastic play, which eventually enabled him to go all the way to the majors, to play third base for the St. Louis, Cardinals, where his salary increased thirty times. Bettger said, "It was what I learned from being fired in the minors that brought my success. Enthusiasm overcame my failure."

Branch Rickey created the minor league farm system to develop young talent in the 1920s. He was then, general manager, for the St. Louis Cardinals, who at that time, had gone nowhere in the baseball world. Minor league clubs operated independently and they developed and sold their players to the major league teams. According to *Smithsonian Q & A*, Rickey had the Cardinals buy thirty-three minor league teams over the years, which became part of the Cardinal organization. His plan of polishing up players, before they ever played one game for the Cardinals, was a success. The Cardinals, who had never won a thing, won five pennants from 1926 to 1934, using players who were developed in their farm system.

In 1942, Branch Rickey was hired by the Dodgers as General Manager. Under Rickey's leadership, the Dodgers organization expanded to become one of the most successful in all of baseball. In ten years, the Brooklyn team won seven pennants between 1947 and 1956. The World Series victory in 1955, was the first for the Dodgers. Since moving to Los Angeles in 1958, their record has been outstanding: six World Championships, eleven Pennants and twenty play-off appearances!

Branch Rickey had a brilliant mind for baseball, along with strong moral and religious convictions. He used his baseball stature to promote ethical values and lifestyles. He was one of the founders of the popular, *Fellowship of Christian Athletes*. The FCA has become a significant factor in helping young people, coaches, their families and others, develop a wholesome and disciplined lifestyle encouraged by churches.

Today, there is more spiritual openness among ball players in general. Baseball players who helped in the founding of FCA were Alvin Dark, Carl Erskine, George Kell, Vernon Law, Bobby Richardson and Brooks Robinson. I have always been proud to say, I played baseball in the farm system of the Dodgers.

The popularity of the minors had peaked in 1949 with forty million fans who watched 450 teams in fifty-nine leagues. But the minor leagues were in big trouble by the mid 1950's. Television which telecasted its first Major League Game on August 1939 was now presenting major league games every day and the big leagues were planning to expand across the continent. To further the woes, the minors were downgraded by regional sports writers and fans. These major catastrophies almost caused the minors to come apart at the seams.

My twin brother Fred and Don Demeter (both former Dodgers) bought the franchise of the Oklahoma City team years ago. The stadium now under new ownership is one of the most beautiful sports facilities for the Triple A Dodgers.

Since the minors were a dying breed at that time, the ball parks were old and in need of much repair. The Sooner State League where I played my first year in the pros was barely hanging on and the only team in the schedule, outside of Oklahoma, Gainsville, Texas, folded early in May. In two short years the Sooner State League, along with the Sunset and Tobacco State Leagues would be faded memories in Baseball history.

When I signed with the Dodger organization, I never gave the declining minors a thought, because staying there was not my goal. They were my personal training ground for the majors. Some call the minors, a "one-way ticket to nowhere," because it's such a long shot to get where you really want to go. Most players never make it and either quit or get released. Only one in fourteen ever make it to the big leagues. In fact, less than ten per-cent of those who sign a pro contract make it to the Big Leagues for even one game.

But, that didn't discourage me, because I was playing my heart's desire. I loved every inning, every endless bus ride and every cheap hotel. Nothing could dampen my spirit, because I was a professional ball player and a Dodger, to boot. For me, it was life at its baseball best.

Beyond a Game

it is a white ball against
a sky so blue it hurts your eyes
it is thick grass, so perfectly green
day fading into evening
Jewel W.

Back in 1955, my first year of pro ball, I pitched for the Dodgers farm team, the Shawnee, Oklahoma Hawks. It was a class D team in the old Sooner State League. Our road trips were taken in an old yellow school bus that on occasions would break down with a flat or some minor repair. In fact, when we finally rolled into Seminole one Saturday afternoon, we were half an hour late for the game. We were pleased to receive an unexpected, enthusiastic applause from the stands.

The big problem, aside from the bumpy rides, was not having air-conditioning. When you are playing in Oklahoma in the summer, the heat index is not your friend. The only good thing about those trips, was our longest, only lasted a couple of hours.

The cheap hotels were something else. The air-conditioned rooms moved the stale air barely more than electric fans. At times, it would stop in the middle of a sultry night. We always looked forward to the trip to Lawton, Oklahoma. The Lawtonian was the newest and best hotel in the league. The air-conditioning was superb! I pitched some of my better games there.

The good thing about those road trips was the daily seven dollar meal money, personally handed to us in cash by our manager, former great relief pitcher for the Dodgers, Jack Banta. The nation's fast-food restaurants had yet to come to those small Oklahoma towns of Shawnee, Muskogee and McAlister. We found local hamburger stops, Chinese noodle places or, if lucky, Italian spaghetti cafés. Actually, we preferred to find a decent place to eat after the game. Banta sold the notion, "a hungry ball player is the best player." Truthfully, it is always better to play on an empty stomach.

The visiting team's club house was no better than high school locker rooms. Consequently, many times we dressed in our hotel room. The only transportation to and from the park was our yellow school bus; so as a team, we stuck pretty close together. You were in bad shape, if you missed the bus!

Actually, the minors are good for fresh ball players living away from home, for the first time. Often the managers were common sense counselors, for green rookies who become home sick or love sick for the girl back home. The biggest adjustments for a rookie is the pressure of playing a game almost every day along with lonesome days and nights on the road. When possible, the parent clubs sent a rookie to a team that was close geographically to his home. As for me, I was disappointed that I went to Shawnee, Oklahoma, instead of Green Bay, Wisconsin. Shawnee was a short drive from Norman, where I went to college at OU. I wanted to see the world!

The lighting in some parks had much to be desired. This was a problem, because we played most of our games at night. The batters, especially, complained of not being able to see the ball clearly. Jack Banta, sometimes shook his head and told us, "Fellows, if you can play ball down here, you can play ball anywhere." As for me, a pitcher, the poor lighting was right up my alley. It was probably one of the reasons I won seventeen games that season!

The two best games I pitched that year were on the road. We beat Seminole, 6-0 in a game where I pitched a one hitter and struck out 15. Four days later in Ponca City, I came off the mound with a 1-0 win, a two hitter and, again, 15 were Ks. My twin, Fred, drove in the winning run with a stand up double. This was the kind of stuff that made me ignore the basic truth of being underpaid, over-worked and enduring the ugliness of the minors, because, there's no ecstasy like winning. For a ball player that's as good as it gets!

In Shawnee, living conditions for single guys was an old rooming house that six of us shared. The bedrooms were upstairs with the kitchen facility downstairs. The cooking amounted to a menu of home-style sandwiches and soft drinks. Later, we moved to a duplex, which was a better arrangement.

The City Cafe on Main Street was our usual hang-out. The owner of the City Café was a real baseball fan and booster. He had a blackboard in the back, near the kitchen, where he left telephone messages and other notes for us. This "answering service" was especially appreciated when we were on the road. So, this was the first place we hit, when we came back to Shawnee.

The only movie theater in town was a block from the City Café, down Main Street. This was a popular place, because we liked the girls who sold tickets and ushered. Our movie going was limited to matinees, since our games were played at night. I enjoyed living in a small city where kids as well as adults knew me by my first name whether on the streets, in shops or at the stadium.

Getting around the town of about 15,000 was a hassle, since most of us did not have the luxury of a car. Even getting to the ball park was an effort, for there was no public transportation and taxi service was too expensive. Usually, we walked the mile to Memorial Stadium.

On our team, we had a rookie pitcher from a farm in Indiana. He was to receive the last of his $4000 bonus, after he stayed with the club for ninety days. He was just like the rubes you read about in baseball history. Our rookie was a country bumpkin, if there ever was one! He thought little Shawnee was big city stuff. His shirt was always hanging out over his baseball pants and his hat never seemed to fit squarely on his head. Unlike the short haircuts most of us wore, his hair hung out in all directions from under his cap. Actually, he was a good, hard throwing pitcher and we felt he could throw a ball through a brick wall!

Our rube was somewhat like the original one. George Rube Waddell was a Hall of Fame left handed pitcher at the beginning of the 1900s. For all of his great pitching for thirteen years he is best remembered for his highly eccentric behavior. He was unpredictable! He would leave the games to chase fire trucks and between seasons he joined a circus to wrestle allegators.

One afternoon, we loaded up to make a trip to Ponca City and couldn't find our hick pitcher. After the mandatory ten minute wait, the bus pulled out without him. This was in late July, ninety-five days into the season. As we were traveling, we heard the continuous blaring of a car horn behind us. Looking out the windows, we saw a car speeding next to our school bus. It was a new, 1955 bright red Pontiac convertible, with beautiful white leather seats. Our rube was driving and waving. He hollered at the top of his lungs, "So long losers, I'm out'ta here!" With that, he sped on past us. We never saw, nor heard of him again. Our rube had jumped the club!

My rookie year record of seventeen wins and six losses, made me feel confident I was on my way to the Bigs. At this point, my call to the ministry was placed on the back burner and baseball had my full attention. Yet today my Dodger baseball uniform number 47 is still a prized possession!

My second year of pro ball was a step up to Class C Pioneer League, in the states of Idaho, Utah and Montana. Our team was flown by the Dodger prop plane from Dodgertown, with one service stop in Nashville, Tennessee, before landing 2,500 miles away in Great Falls, Montana. This Dodger affiliate team was called by its new name, The Electrics, because of the many power plants in the area.

Our stadium, Legion Field, held about 3200 spectators, much larger than Shawnee's Memorial stadium. It was situated in the shadow of grain elevators and the tallest smoke stack in the world. This was "Big Sky Country," with western skies stretching across the great high plains. The fans of that pioneer city greeted us royally. Instantly, I liked what I saw and the atmosphere of the West. I said to myself, "Now, this is more like it." I was seeing the world!

To my surprise, we were snowed out of our first five games, but we knew we were in for a great summer of baseball. Many times, we would say that old baseball cliché "No runs, no hits, no errors" and then add, "and some are rained out." But who ever heard of being snowed out?

Baseball Haiku

Nine men stand waiting
Under storm clouds that gather.
Someone asks for time.
Ron Vazzano

During those home game rainouts and early season snow outs, we cashed in on the Great Falls business community's coupons and certificates that were given to us. These perks from specialty clothing stores, department stores and restaurants were for our baseball feats on the field. This brightened up those rainouts and took away some of the discouragement of being more than 2000 miles from Brooklyn's Ebbets Field.

Mark J. Mitchel must have spent some time in the Big Sky country playing professional ball when he wrote:

"Minor league rain-outs
in Montana.
No sun only gray sky.
Waiting for the wind
to slow down
and the rains to end.
The game was holy
and the rain sacred."

Norman Rockwell's famous painting, "Bottom of the Sixth," first appeared on the cover of the *Saturday Evening Post*, in April, 1949, showing three umpires standing together in Brooklyn's Ebbets Field. They are looking up at a cloudy sky, with the hand of the plate umpire, trying to catch a larger than life raindrop.

My Day

It was my day
To go out to play.

I got my glove
My baseball bat
Got my ball
And baseball cap.

I threw the ball
Up in the air,
Scared two birds
Sitting there.

Grabbed my bat
Took a mighty swing,
Threw up the ball
And missed the thing.

Bat on my shoulder
Jugglin' the ball,
I yelled out loud
"Where are y'all?"

I whistled real loud
And hollered a bit,
I never gave up
I never quit.
Johnny came out
Without his glove,
He pointed up
To the sky above.

Then Frank and Bobby
Did the same,
Shaking their heads
There'd be no game.

The clouds rolled in
With drops of rain.
I thought of baseball
From my window pane.

No sense crying
No sense to pout,
Some games get delayed
Some get rained out.
Fred D. Minton, Ph.D.

Ball players have a lot of time on their hands during the day, since ninety percent of games are played under the lights. A lot of guys are movie hounds, some like to hang out and play cards or shoot pool; a few of us who had yet to graduate from college, studied correspondence courses. Since, we knew deep down, only a handful of us had a chance for big time baseball, we gave serious thought to life outside of pro ball. Paul Stamen, our catcher, was planning to be an attorney. Bill Brown had connections in Great Falls and spent a good deal of time with businessmen in the area. I knew before I signed my contract, God had called me to preach the Gospel, so finishing my college was a step into the future.

When our team was on the road, after checking into the hotel, I looked up the Southern Baptist Churches in the yellow pages. I enjoyed getting acquainted with the local pastors and most of the time, we had lunch together. On one occasion, in Twin Falls, Idaho, the small congregation was constructing a building in which to worship. In fact, the pastor, Harold Dillman, was literally building it himself. My twin brother and I decided to help, so for two afternoons, we dug footings and poured concrete. When it came time for the game, we could hardly drag ourselves onto the field. Our hands were so blistered, holding a bat was painful. Our aches and pains were for the Kingdom of God, so we thought it was worth it.

After arriving in Great Falls we found the same big problem. The city of 45,000 didn't have any public transportation. Most of our team rented rooms near downtown in the large home of widowed Mrs. Ball. But we still had to go back and forth to the stadium, which was at the edge of the city near the great Missouri River which has five spectacular falls. Some guys had girlfriends who got their dad's car. Five of us bought a green Ford and split the cost. We parked the car downtown and whoever found it, drove it. It was not a good plan. It didn't take long before second baseman, John Etheridge from Sundown, Texas and I, bought the other guys out and confiscated the keys. We did give our teammates free taxi service to the ball field.

Playing in the great Northwest was a new experience for most of my teammates and it was a problem for some to get acclimated. The guys from the South were never happy with the hamburgers, which were served without lettuce, tomatoes, pickles or mustard. The local hamburgers came with only catsup and onions. Players from California seemed to do better in the new world around them. One teammate complained, "They don't even say hello or thank you." One fan said, "We're not rude, we just don't waste words like you guys from the South." I was fortunate to have played semi-pro ball in South Dakota one summer with the Oklahoma University summer team, which had prepared me for this rugged lifestyle.

The best upgrade was our transportation. We had a genuine air-conditioned Greyhound travel bus for all our trips and trips we took! The pioneer league was made up of cities in three of the largest states in America: Idaho, Utah and Montana. Our closest city was Missoula, Montana which was a four or five hour drive. Our longest trip, was to the largest city, Salt Lake City, Utah, an eight hour journey. Our bus had a customized bed in the rear for the starting pitcher to sleep on overnight travels. During some of those long tiring trips, I took the risk and climbed into the over-head luggage space to stretch out my legs and sleep. The scenery was so spectacular; the trips were "National Geographic" photo snaps.

We had a great bunch, which were chosen from spring training by our manager, Lou Rochelle. I thought this was going to be a winning year, but it just didn't happen. It was during this season, my twin was sent to another club. This was the first time in our lives we were separated in baseball. Our team's season was dismal, with a 64 – 68 record, ending in sixth place in an eight team league. My pitching record was just as discouraging with a 6 - 5 record.

The only bright spot for me was, I won two games on the same day. We had a split double-header in a home stand at Legion Stadium. We won the first game, 3-1 and I was the winning pitcher of record. There was a planned four hour delay before the night cap. With the score tied, Lou Rochelle, asked how my arm felt and when I responded eagerly, he put me in to relieve. It was the seventh inning with the game tied 3-3. Fortunately, we got the needed run and I came out the winning pitcher, again.

My third year, the Dodgers sent me to Reno, Nevada, in the Class C, California State League. This was a step up from the Pioneer League even though both leagues had the same classification. Since the Dodgers planned move to Los Angeles the next year, our proximity gave our team better access to big league scouting.

Travel, hotels, restaurants, stadiums and ball parks were all upgraded. The road meal money was increased to fifteen dollars a day, which was given to us in cash at the beginning of the trip. It is interesting, the ball clubs, who came to play us, received their meal money only one day at a time, due to the open gambling in Reno.

We had a great manager, Ray "Little Buffalo" Perry. He had played in the Pacific Coast League and probably would have been a solid Major Leaguer had he not broken his leg. He knew baseball! Our second place 1957 Reno Silver Sox team, had four players out of sixteen team members who moved up to play in the majors. They were: Doug Camilli, catcher; Bob Gialombardo, left handed pitcher; Charlie Smith, shortstop; and Nat Smith, catcher. When only one minor leaguer out of fourteen ever reaches the majors you can see our Reno team was loaded with talent. "Little Buffalo," knew how to pick prime prospects from spring training to put together this winning ball club.

I was fortunate to have Joyce with me during my third year of baseball and our honeymoon first year of marriage. I remember how anxious I was when she watched me pitch, for the first time, as a professional. Even though, she had seen me pitch a few times in high school, this was a whole new ball game. In our first home game, I came in as a relief pitcher in the seventh inning. As I pitched, I spotted my beauty in the stands. And then, threw each pitch like it was a World Series! I was grateful that I did a good relief save for the win! Afterward, I asked her if she was nervous about watching me pitch. She answered with her usual calmness, "Not really, I thought anything you got yourself into, you were big enough to get yourself out." Little did she know!

Minor league baseball wives have tough times keeping the home fires burning, while their husband goes after his dream. Some wives are not able to move to be with their husband for the season, because the money is not available. As Hall of Famer, Carl Erskine recalls in his book, *Tales from the Dodger Dugout*, "While baseball players are trying to raise their batting averages and pitchers are trying to lower their earned run averages, wives are busy trying to raise their kids and doing chores at home. However, that doesn't exempt a baseball wife from the frayed nerves and anxious moments of game."

On our second road trip to Fresno, California, I planned to buy a new business suit. Some guys on the team knew of a men's specialty clothing store that had quality suits at a good price. On the way, I passed a jewelry store and there, in the window was a beautiful white gold heart shaped necklace, with a diamond at the top. It caught my eye! Since this was our honeymoon year, I couldn't resist bringing it home to my bride.

All of our daughters, Lori, Lisa, Lesli and our daughter-in-law, Kristie, have worn it at their wedding. It is a sentimental keepsake. Joyce holds it second, only to her wedding ring. Every time she wears that necklace, it reminds me of my love for her and my love for baseball. It's a love thing.

In late July, while pitching, my left shoulder began to ache after a few innings. At that juncture of the season I had registered ten wins against only one loss. Instead of complaining, I tried to endure and kept on pitching without rest, because the size of our team roster was limited; all of us were ready to be called upon to play any position. Pinch hitters and pinch runners were usually supplied by pitchers. There was no such thing as a "prima donna" on the club. We did it all.

Pitchers were expected to go the entire game, if at all possible. It cost me and our team because, at times, my pitching became very ineffective. I knew we were very thin in our pitching ranks, so I continued. It was a bad decision for me and the team. We ended up second in the league; I won only four more games that season, with my record slipping to fourteen wins and six losses. I needed those few days of rest, for after the season ended, my left shoulder no longer hurt.

All along the way, in my three years in the minors, I found each league had its own characteristic. Fans were reflections of their part of the country.

The fans at the games in The Sooner State League, gave evidences of folks with a small town and country flavor. Cowboy hats, sprinkled the stands and were mostly well worn straws. It was a working class of people, with a down- home, friendly openness. They came to enjoy a game, win or lose.

In the Pioneer League, the fans were more boisterous and demonstrative about their baseball. Many western hats were worn by ranchers with nice clothes and fine boots. They seemed to be more aware of the scope of the game and much more intense about its outcome. They did not like to lose. Winning was expected, in fact, the stands emptied rather quickly, if the score became too lopsided. Even so, the fans treated the players with warm regard and almost star status.

One of the most precious treasures I have kept to remind me of my baseball days is a letter from a nine year old boy printed on a school note book paper.

DEAR MR. MINTON,

THANK YOU FOR YOUR BASEBALL
YOU SIGNED FOR ME.
I WANT TO TELL PEOPLE ABOUT GOD
LIKE YOU DO.

SINCERELY, JOSHUA

The California State league brought a big city atmosphere. Reno's famous banner across its main street said it all, for cities in our league, "The Biggest Little City in the World." The fans considered themselves sophisticated, big city people. The ball games were not the only ticket in town; the spectators had a lot of choices. Good baseball was expected and proximity to Major League cities put pressure on the league to field good, competitive teams.

However, there is nothing that compares to the home city in which you play. It doesn't take long, before it becomes home. Those small ball parks bring you closer to your fans, because the fans are closer to the playing field.

Moana Park - Reno , Nevada (1957).

This gives an approachable atmosphere, like family. They walked by and said, "Hi Frank, I'm glad you're pitching tonight." What a great feeling. It's not fame or fortune, just good home town friendliness. Memorial Park – Shawnee, Oklahoma, Legion Stadium - Great Falls, Montana, Moana Park – Reno, Nevada; all three bring warm memories of home.

David Lamb in his terrific Article, "A season in the Minors" in the National Geographic" In those little ball parks, I found moments of shared summer leisure and time to dream of the days when I was young and all great feats were possible. The world about me had changed, yet everything was exactly as I had remembered it, the games rules, the language of the fans, the rituals on the field, event the soft glow of June nights."

His thoughts gives me sentimental memory of my baseball days in the minors in the 1950's. I am grateful, God granted it!

Church is similar and a whole lot more. Almost everyone is greeted with a down home "Hello" and a hardy handshake. In most churches you're only a stranger once. The relaxed atmosphere takes away the old formal "churchy stuff" of the past. The wonderful thing is, Jesus is present. He said, "Where two or three are gathered together in my name, I am there among them."

One evening, when I was eleven years old, I was walking with my year older sister Marlene and my twin brother, Fred by the Wellington Place Baptist Church in Wichita, Kansas. The folks were singing and the music spilled out onto the street. With nothing more to do, we scampered in and sat in the back. There were about one hundred people present and when the congregation stopped singing, the pastor, Dr. Vernon Reffner came to the pulpit and preached. It was then and there, I asked Jesus to come into my heart. After the last prayer and "A-men," we were the first ones out the door and hurried to grandma's house.

I never felt alone again, for I knew of God's presence in my life. His promise, "I will never leave you nor forsake you," was one I held deep in my heart. Throughout my baseball career, I knew He was there when I pitched.

It was August 17 and getting along in the baseball season. This was the time for every player to be at his best. The year had given us more experience and expertise. My pitching season at Great Falls was lack luster at best (6 wins 5 losses)

With determination I was ready to pitch my very best but for some reason I threw the ball everywhere except over the plate, it seemed that everything I threw was just a bunch of junk. Not at all like me. I was devastated! Out of the dugout came manager Lou Rochell, "Stop thinking Minton, You're hurting the club!" No excuse, my mound workout was over for the day.

Into the dugout I strode and then to the locker room. After an early shower I sat in silence almost dazed. When the game was over the team trooped in. I just couldn't stand being a loser so I put a towel over my head and cried, like a baby.

Lou seeing his pathetic pitcher said, "Guys if all of you would take a loss like Minton we would win the league!" All for one and one for all. Pats on the back and words of encouragement didn't change anything but it eased my hurting heart for the long trip home. As the bus traveled in the night, I quietly remembered the words of Jesus, "I will never leave you nor forsake you." Those words were already lodged in my heart the night when I gave my life to Jesus.

According to David Lamb, *National Geographic*, "After a long slump, minor league baseball is on the upswing." Today, the minors are a long way from being dead. Two minor league stadiums are being planned for the Houston, Texas, area. A 4,500 capacity stadium is on the drawing boards to be built by 2012 along U.S. 59 in Montgomery County, north of Houston.

Another stadium with a 10,000 capacity, is planned in the Katy corridor, west of Houston, to be built and be operational, also, in 2012. Brooks Robinson, former St. Louis Cardinal, great, is the driving force behind this endeavor.

Joyce and I with life long friends, John and Aldine Bisagno enjoyed a baseball evening watching, "the Skeeters" play in their new stadium built in 2013 along the Katy, Texas corridor.

Houston is not alone in large metro areas getting minor league teams in the near future. The Denver, Colorado area has two commitments, for teams to play in new stadiums, which are to be built within two years. The newly built minor league stadium in San Jose, California, is state of the art, with sky boxes, play grounds for children, major restaurants and large screens to feature replay action.

Flying on Southwest Airlines into New Orleans, I sat next to a real minor league baseball fan, J.D. Vinson. He has season tickets to the triple-A Pacific Coast, New Orleans Zephyrs, which play in their 12,500 capacity stadium. He keeps up with the majors, but his enthusiasm is for the minors.

His conversation really picked up, when talking about the Class double-A Montgomery, Alabama, Biscuits, who are in the Southern League. When J.D. is in Montgomery, he always takes in a Biscuit game, because the 7,000 capacity Riverwalk Stadium is right downtown. I was especially interested, when he told me about the team's mascot, "Monty," who is an anthropomorphized buttermilk biscuit. The costumed "Monty," shoots wrapped, edible biscuits, with an air cannon, into the eager crowd. Vinson said, "They have all kinds of biscuits for sale at the park. It's like hot dog sales in other places."

There is something very personal and inspiring for smaller cities and suburban communities to be provided with live, professional baseball. A minor league team is a farm source for the bigs and cultivates future stars that give civic pride.

In the Bible, there was a minor league disciple, who did a major league ministry in the work of God. Even though Andrew, was one of the first to be called, he was still a minor leaguer, in the sense he was not in the "inner circle" with Jesus' major three; Peter, James and John. His name is not mentioned in the Bible without the tag, "Simon Peter's brother," thus indicating his second standing.

Even though relegated to a minor league role, he made three great major league plays. When he found Jesus, he immediately brought his brother Simon Peter to him. Andrew later brought to Jesus a boy who shared his lunch of five loaves of bread and two fish. Jesus multiplied the boy's offering to feed the crowd of five thousand. In Andrew's minor role, he made a major move by introducing the Greeks to Jesus. This brought the outside world to hear the Gospel. Simply put, Andrew did the work of the Lord in a Major League way.

When I was pastor of Far Hills Baptist church, a large congregation in Dayton, Ohio, a fine family man in his early thirties, a member of our congregation, came to my study. He revealed, God had called him to preach. His quiet and shy nature made me question his call to serve the Lord as a preacher. I did my best to explain to him that very few have the opportunity to pastor a large city church, like ours. I thought, perhaps, he may have been struck with a "major league" church syndrome.

"Oh no, pastor," he said, "not me, in a big church pulpit. I just want to prepare myself for a small country church somewhere." He moved his family to Fort Worth, Texas, to attend Southwestern Baptist Theological Seminary. I have always marveled and appreciated his willingness to serve as a "minor leaguer" for Jesus. He had the true servant's heart.

Jesus said, "A businessman was on big trip. He was going to be gone for a long time and needed to trust employees with his properties. When he returned, he praised the first one. "Well done, good and trustworthy caretaker, you have been faithful with a few things, I will put you in charge of many things. Come and share my happiness." I believe that God has the same blessing for this faithful country preacher.

Go tell it on the mountain,
Over the hills and ev'rywhere;
Go tell it on the mountain,
That Jesus Christ is born.
John W. Work, Jr.
African-American folk melody

CHAPTER 8

SWING AND GO FOR BROKE!

Casey at the Bat

The outlook wasn't brilliant for the Mudville nine that day:
The score stood four to two with but one inning more to play.
And then when Cooney died at first, and Barrows did the same,
A sickly silence fell upon the patrons of the game.

A straggling few got up to go in deep despair. The rest
Clung to that hope which springs eternal in the human breast;
They thought if only Casey could but get a whack at that—
We'd put up even money, now, with Casey at the bat.

But Flynn preceded Casey, as did also Jimmy Blake,
And the former was a lulu and the latter was a cake;
So upon the stricken multitude grim melancholy sat,
For there seemed but little chance of Casey's getting to the bat.

But Flynn let drive a single, to the wonderment of all,
And Blake, the much despised, tore the cover off the ball;
And when the dust had lifted, and the men saw what had occurred,
There was Johnnie safe at second and Flynn a-hugging third.

Then from 5,000 throats and more there rose a lusty yell;
It rumbled through the valley, it rattled in the dell;
It knocked upon the mountain and recoiled upon the flat,
For Casey, mighty Casey, was advancing to the bat.

There was ease in Casey's manner as he stepped into his place;
There was pride in Casey's bearing and a smile on Casey's face.
And when, responding to the cheers, he lightly doffed his hat,
No stranger in the crowd could doubt 'twas Casey at the bat.

Ten thousand eyes were on him as he rubbed his hands with dirt;
Five thousand tongues applauded when he wiped them on his shirt.
Then while the writhing pitcher ground the ball into his hip,
Defiance gleamed in Casey's eye, a sneer curled Casey's lip.

And now the leather-covered sphere came hurtling through the air
And Casey stood a-watching it in haughty grandeur there.
Close by the sturdy batsman the ball unheeded sped –
"That ain't my style," said Casey. "Strike one," the umpire said.

From the benches, black with people, there went up a muffled roar,
Like the beating of the storm-waves on a stern and distant shore.
"Kill him! Kill the umpire!" shouted some one on the stand;
And it's likely they'd have killed him had not Casey raised his hand.

With a smile of Christian charity great Casey's visage shone;
He stilled the rising tumult; he bade the game go on;
He signaled to the pitcher, and once more the spheroid flew;
But Casey still ignored it, and the umpire said, "Strike two."

"Fraud!" cried the maddened thousands, and echo answered fraud;
But one scornful look from Casey and the audience was awed.
They saw his face grow stern and cold, they saw his muscles strain,
And they knew that Casey wouldn't let that ball go by again.

The sneer is gone from Casey's lip, his teeth are clenched in hate;
He pounds with cruel violence his bat upon the plate.
And now the pitcher holds the ball, and now he lets it go,
And now the air is shattered by the force of Casey's blow.

Oh, somewhere in this favored land the sun is shining bright;
The band is playing somewhere and somewhere hearts are light,
And somewhere men are laughing, and somewhere children shout;
But there is no joy in Mudville – mighty Casey has struck out.
Ernest Lawrence Thayer

CASEY AT THE bat has been immortalized ever since that beloved poem was printed in the *San Francisco Examiner* in 1888. It has become the most famous poem of baseball and Mudville has become symbolic of all towns and cities, whose fans have had their hearts broken. The home run slugger had his chance to send his home town fans away with happy hearts, "But there is no joy in Mudville – mighty Casey has Struck Out." If Thayer had ended his story with Casey hitting the anticipated home run, his poem would probably have "died on third."

In the early days of baseball most home runs were inside the park with the hitter running around the bases as fast as he could. There were no balls clearing the fence. The type of ball used did not give the "smack" needed for the batter to knock it out of the park. The "power game" came later beginning with the new ball bringing in the Ruth era.

The new ball was made possible by the manufacturing processes that tightened up the yarn and the use of better rubber materials. The ball itself had a harder surface for the horsehide to stretch over. All of this gave the ball a better bounce when it was hit. The time was ripe for the popular home run races to begin!

In my lifetime there have been three exciting home run races. The first was in 1961 with Mickey Mantle and Roger Maris, the M & M Boys. The second, Hank Aaron's 1974 chase of Babe Ruth's all time record 714 home runs. The third race was between Mark McGuire and Sammy Sosa in 1998. For me, all three of these races overshadowed everything else that happened in baseball during those years. These three races became national obsessions. People who normally didn't pay much attention to baseball, got very interested.

The home run race between Roger Maris and Mickey Mantle was unique because they were Yankee teammates. Throughout the season, when the Yankees came to any city, the race came with them. Fans were thrilled they could see the race in person.

When the Kansas City Royals hosted the New York Yankees, it was extra special for me. Since I was pastoring a mission church in nearby Atchison, Kansas and attending Midwestern Baptist Seminary in Kansas City, I jumped at the chance to go to the game. Joyce and I got seats high up in the third tier along the first base line. It was like reaching back into my past and once again feeling I belonged to the game. I was rooting for Mickey Mantle to hit one out that night, but it was Maris who came through.

This race ended with Maris' historic 61 home runs, breaking Babe Ruth's record of 60. I believe that Mantle's close pursuit pushed Maris to break the Babe's record. Late in the season Mickey hurt his leg again which slowed his home run production to 54. Even though it took Maris longer to break the record (162 games, compared to the great Bambino's 154 games), it was a race to be remembered.

The pressure of the race took its toll on Roger. His hair came out in clumps and every time he hit one, goose pimples would break out all over his skin. When asked what his feelings were after he broke the record he told the press, "As a ball player, I would be delighted to do it again. As an individual, I doubt if I could possibly go through it again."

Then in 1974, all eyes were upon Hank Aaron of the Atlanta Braves as he was about to make baseball history approaching the Babe's lifetime record of 714 home runs. I was pastor of the Far Hills Baptist Church in Dayton, Ohio at that time, so it was my pleasure to take in some more baseball history. It was the opening game of the season and in Cincinnati, that is always a sellout. A record crowd of 52,150 poured into River Front Stadium that April fifth afternoon and the scalpers were doing a flourishing business outside the gates. Joyce and I were fortunate to have tickets, so we didn't mind being in the upper deck on the third level to watch this game.

It was an excited, overflow crowd who loved their Reds. This exceptional team led by Johnny Bench, George Foster, Joe Morgan and Pete Rose brought home two World Championships in the following years of 1975 and 1976. Thus the combination of Hank Aaron's mystique along with the soon to be World Champions made it a game, never to be forgotten.

Hank was only one home run away from tying Ruth's record and he didn't disappoint us! He sent a Jack Billingham three ball, one strike pitch over the left center wall some 375 feet away. Tom Stanton in his fine book *Hank Aaron,* so aptly summarized, "Hank Aaron had tied Babe Ruth on his first swing of the season." And the Minton family saw it with all four children!

We all stood in the packed River Front stadium cheering and honoring Hank Aaron as he gave his familiar, humble, yet victorious, jog around the bases. It truly was a historic achievement that connected us all to the great Bambino.

The nervous Braves management sighed with relief that Hank did not hit another home run the rest of the weekend series. They wanted the next home run to be hit at home. Hank didn't disappoint them! On April eighth, 1974, in Atlanta, Georgia, he broke the record in the fourth inning, his second at bat with a 385 foot shot into the left field bullpen off the Dodgers left hander, Al Downing.

Hank went on to finish his illustrious career in 1976 smashing 755 home runs. Even though Aaron was just an average sized ball player, he swung that 33.5 inch, 34.75 ounce white ash bat with authority. He was nicknamed "Mr. Consistency" because Hank hit 20 or more home runs for 20 consecutive years. If any hitter deserved the right to break Babe Ruth's record, the honor deservedly went to Hank. He earned it! I shall always admire his baseball lifestyle for it had a certain grace about it. The more I research the life of the man, the more admiration I have for him. In a TV interview Hank said, "It's more timing than anything else. You don't have to be real big. Time it right and the ball will go far enough"

When he was a boy, Hank was too poor to own a bat. He learned to play baseball in a pecan grove in his hometown of Mobile, Alabama. He had unusual strength in his arms because as a teenager he worked on an ice truck. He left home with two sandwiches, two dollars and two pair of pants in a cardboard suitcase.

Hank lived 86 productive years and walked with the Lord. His genuine humility blessed all of us.

"My life is to give back. God has been good to me so I share with others." With talk of his consistent home run hitting he concluded, "Success in life is taking one step at a time."

Recently, I saw an old black and white footage of one of the first televised Home Run Derbies. Hank won the contest and throughout the many interviews that day, his demeanor was gracious and kind to those he beat. In his own words from his autobiography, after breaking Ruth's record, he gave us an inside look at his heart when he wrote, "I got down on my knees and closed my eyes and thanked God for pulling me through."

The third home run race of great interest was in 1998 between Mark McGuire, first baseman with the St Louis Cardinals and Sammy Sosa, outfielder for the Chicago Cubs. Headlines in the news kept the power race before us as home runs were belted game after game. The entire nation responded with a renewed interest in baseball that had been marred by the 1994 strike.

Yet, with all of this hype and scrutiny something didn't seem right. Even though both players had shown prowess at the plate in the past, it seemed surreal that both players were approaching unbelievable slugging records. Younger players usually are the ones who show such power, but these men were past their prime. Was it a souped-up ball manufactured by the Rawlings Company? What was happening? Did these players deserve the national attention? To our disappointment this race brought confusion and finally the pallor of suspected drug use. Instead of glory, Mark McGwire's 70, and Sammy Sosa's 66, home runs brought clouds of doubt and huge questions to the game America loved.

The stadium faces blur
in the afternoon sun.
The celebration ends
in the afternoon sun.
The victory becomes defeat
in the afternoon sun.

The death of honor.
The end of a fading
and final trust,
of too many afternoons
in too many suns.
Anonymous
Chicago Times 1919

In the aftermath of all the home run hype, the 409 page Mitchell Report was released December 13, 2007. The report brought by Senator George

J. Mitchell was the result of a twenty-one month investigation into performance-enhancing drug use in Major League baseball. Eighty-nine players were named in the investigation, who allegedly used steroids or drugs. The Major League baseball union attempted to delay its findings, but a few of the well-known players' names did leak out at the beginning. The baseball bombshell was shocking! But Baseball needed it.

Jesus also shocked the religious world with his only act of physical aggressiveness. "Jesus went into the temple's outer court and drove out all those buying and selling in the temple. He overturned the money changers' tables and the chairs of those selling doves.

And he said to them, 'It is written, my house will be called a house of prayer. But you are making it a den of thieves'."

The people's gifts of money and animal sacrifices were being rejected by the temple guardians. Therefore, people were forced to pay higher prices for "temple approved" coins and animal sacrifices. To make matters worse, the little birds or doves brought by the poor were also denied acceptance. It was a racket! The people accepted Jesus' astonishing display because they knew his actions were needed. The courtyard procedures which allowed thievery and hindered prayer were a flagrant violation of worship.

To me, baseball was about to forfeit integrity and lower its' standards to become, "The Show" instead of "The Game". The last thing any thinking person in the baseball world would suggest, is that the game is a show. The word show implies prearrangement and rehearsal. I believe it would destroy true competiveness and eventually the game itself. Jose Canseco, super outfielder for twenty-one years (1985-2001), was dubbed, "The Chemist." In his book, *Juiced,* he openly stated, "I was an entertainer for the Show. Fans just want to have fun at the ball park." Jose's reputation has rebounded somewhat, however, he is still confused as to what baseball is all about. I'm comforted that he is no longer in the game.

John Smallwood, of the *Philadelphia Daily News* warns, "Major League Baseball has moved away from the world of sports and into the world of sports entertainment, and just like in wrestling entertainment, nothing that happens can truly be believed."

Steroid use has raised its ugly head and I agree wholeheartedly with Smallwood, it could ruin our national pastime. Will we now question all those past records that are celebrated in The Hall of Fame in Cooperstown? You find yourself wondering, "What does baseball believe in or stand for, if anything?

Moving hopefully away from steroids, we now face the Houston Astros sign stealing scandal, it began in the 2017 season and continued as they won the 2019 World Series against the Los Angeles Dodgers, using their secret.

The players would get the signal of the pitch from a centerfield camera feed that decoded what pitch selection by the catcher, when giving the pitcher a sign as to what pitch he was to deliver. The player on the bench banged on a trash can lid with a bat for a curve on an off speed pitch. A fast ball received no sound.

This took the element of surprise from the batter as to the pitch that was coming. A big advantage for the batter! With the start of the 2021 season fans and opposing team players have not forgotten this unfair scheme that was used against them. On May 26,2021 when the Dodgers played the Astros at Houston's Minute maid Park, Hundreds of Dodger fans came to protest in retaliation.

From time to time they would stand and boo throughout the game. During the game a number of fights occurred. No one was tossed and no one was arrested. Some now call H-towns nickname, "Trash Town" for the Astros use of a trash can lid banging from the dugout to signal the coming pitch.

Commissioner Manfred fined the team $5 million the maximum allowed by the MLB constitution and revolked their first and second round draft pick in 2020 and 2021.

No Astro players were punished because they received immunity in exchange for their cooperation in the investigation. Now as I watch the Astros play, I am reminded what the Bible says "Be sure your sins will find you out" but it also says "Be kind and compassionate to one another, forgiving each other" so Take me out to the ball game" in Houston, Texas!

America without baseball, could it ever be? With baseball gone, what would America feel and do and see? Good ole' baseball vernacular would become a lost art. "Knock it out'ta the park, three strikes you're out, kill the umpire and don't die on third," would become unintelligible gibberish. Spring would bring its April showers, May flowers and chiggers, but no spring training. Would there be hope of a "Second Coming" of America's Pastime? The daily sports page would be lacking and the stadiums empty remnants of what had been. Baseball would have killed itself with cheating, greed and steroids, in an effort to produce a show that would spin the turnstiles faster and faster. Baseball's pride and glory, The Hall of Fame, would be buried and forgotten, if the day came that baseball died. Warning! Danger! High Explosive! The heart and soul of baseball is at stake!

Its players like Albert Pujols, the Babe Ruth of our day, who will help redeem baseball. In a personal interview concerning steroids, he told *Sports Illustrated* writer Joe Posnanski, "We are under a dark cloud and nobody believes anything players say. I fear God too much to do anything like that." Albert went on to back up his words, "I don't want to be remembered as the best baseball player ever. I want to be remembered as a great guy who loved the Lord, loved to serve the community and who gave back. That's the guy I want to be remembered as, when I'm done wearing this uniform. That's from the bottom of my heart."

Baseball can breathe a little better now with the public acknowledgement of Mike McGwire, stating by telephone to Ronald Blum AP sports writer, "I'm coming clean and being honest, it's the first time they've heard me talk about this. I hid it from everybody." He repeatedly expressed regret for his decision to use steroids, which he said was "foolish. I wish I had never played in the steroid era."

The Houston Chronicle, January 12, 2010 quoted Astro's first baseman, Lance Berkman. "I think it's good that he came out and admitted it. It's good for him and good for the sport. It hopefully will get us out of this mess. It's been a black eye for the sport." Lance retired as one of the greatest switch hitters in baseball, and is the baseball coach for Houston's Baptist University Baseball team.

In my opinion as a former baseballer, Barry Bonds stole the homerun crown from Hank Aaron with his tainted steroid 762 round trippers. It is sad for Bonds and pitcher Roger Clemens who must live in the shadows of what could have been instead of the light as Hall of Famers.

The Bible speaks in Ecclesiastes of "A time to weep." We baseball fans must agree that time has come. I think it is good that the Hall of Fame has yet to elect McGuire to that prestigious forum. In my opinion, steroid users and gamblers should never be given that honor.

To protect the honor of past players, The Hall of Fame must never lower its standards that has given baseball a secular sacredness. Records, they say are made to be broken, but not with steroids or other artificial enhancements. In my opinion, steroid enhanced records should have question marks or asterisks in big letters in *The Book*. Yes, as we say in Texas, "BIG AS DALLAS!" Plain and simple, the use of steroids is cheating. It will destroy any sport. Fair play is the essence of sports.

In 1919 baseball experienced gambling big time when eight players including star Joe Jackson of the Chicago White Sox (Branded the Black sock) threw the World Series fixed by gamblers. All eight players were banned for life. Perhaps the plea of a little boy sitting on the court steps as Joe Jackson walked by "Say it ain't so Joe, Say it ain't so!" touched the heart strings of America. As Ken Burns writes, "America is about second chances, of hope and renewal. We love come back stories and the prodigal son that Jesus told." The movie, "Field of Dreams" gives hope. Yet we know that gambling will destroy any sport including baseball.

Shame on the Supreme court of America giving the go ahead on sports gambling! Lucky Pete Rose!

I believe "Baseball has done more to move America in the right direction than politics" but I know that only Christianity can win America back to God! I mights add, baseball has defined America.

Regardless of the outcome, as Smallwood wrote in spring of 2009, "Bonds will never be treated with the reverence of Henry Aaron or Babe Ruth. Clemens won't be remembered with the same grace as pitchers like Walter Johnson, Sandy Koufax and Tom Seaver. A-Rod, no matter how incredible his final statistics, will never be mentioned in the same breath as Willie Mays or Mickey Mantle."

Cheating and lying happened in Bible times too. Barnabas, a godly man, sold some property and gave the entire amount he had received to the church. A couple, Ananias and his wife Sapphira, also wanted the praise of the congregation. They sold some of their property for a certain amount but kept part of it back for themselves. When bringing the gift of money to the church, they indicated they were giving the full amount. Their deceit was found out. The apostle Peter said, "Wasn't the money at your disposal? What made you think of doing such a thing? You have not lied to men but to God."

In November 2009, I was blessed to watch the televised testimony of one of the greatest comebacks in baseball history. Josh Hamilton testified of "going from tattoos, to drugs and steroids, to finally being suspended for a year from all of baseball and not playing a game for three years." The great Texas Ranger home run slugging outfielder shamefully continued, "I got to the place, I didn't care about anything but me." Humbly, he explained his victory was through the prayer and daily caring, his grandmother gave him, "She showed me the light at the end of that terrible dark tunnel. She encouraged me to go to the Betty Ford Drug Rehab Center, but even with that help, it took giving all of my drug life over to God."

Josh continued speaking to the overflow home coming crowd, in the Athens Drive High School gym, in Raleigh, North Carolina. Everyone listened intently as he poured out his heart, concluding, "I had to get right with the Lord!" When he ended his sincere speech, the crowd spontaneously stood, clapped and gave a cheering ovation.

God has honored Josh's repentance by allowing him to have a legendary 2010 season, with the Texas Rangers. Tom Verducci, sports writer for, *Inside Baseball*, declares, "In the snapshot of today's game, based on skill set and production, right now, Hamilton is the new BPB, Best Player in Baseball."

Jesus, out of a heart of love warns, "For what good is it for a man to gain the whole world yet forfeit his own soul? Or what can a man give in exchange for his soul?" The desire to get that extra edge cannot be compared with a satisfied mind and heart.

My dad was a country western big fan. When he came home from the stock yards where he was a cattle broker, he would turn on the radio to hear his favorite singer, Hank Williams.

Money can't buy back
Youth when your old,
Nor a heart that is broken
Or a love that's gone cold
The wealthiest person,
Is a pauper like kind
Compared to the man
With a satisfied mind

Country Western Melody

MINTON AT THE BAT

Wichita, Kansas North high school student newspaper, The Star.

Chapter 9
BASEBALL AT ITS BEST

I consider myself
To be the luckiest man
On the face of the earth!
Lou Gehrig
July 4, 1939

It's ball players like Albert Pujols, Lance Berkman and present MVP Jose Altuve, of the 2017 World Series Houston Astros, who give us hope that the steroid dilemma will be behind us and the thrill of the home run will once again feel genuine. Then, the yearly honest home run race will eclipse the clouded past. Babe Ruth's home runs overcame the Chicago Black Socks gambling scandal in 1919 and saved baseball from utter ruin. So I say, "Do it again, baseball, do it again!"

Home runs and Babe Ruth will always be synonymous with baseball at its best, regardless of those players who surpass his record. According to Daniel Okrent's, *Baseball Anecdotes,* "The fans who actually watched Babe Ruth play said, No one could hit 'em like the Bambino and no one could strike out like him. No one ever hit them with more style and drama than the Babe. He was electrifying even when he swung and missed. His missed swing would propel his body almost completely around, twisting his legs like a pretzel. Because of this tremendous display of power, he became famous as the 'Sultan of Swat' and they dubbed the old Yankee Stadium, 'The House that Ruth Built.' Whether it was a home run or a strike out, it was all with a flamboyant flair."

It was my turn to bat
and I hit the ball
So that it sailed
Right over the wall,
I started to run
How happy I'd be
if my team won
First base, second,
Third-I'm home free!
Hurrah for my team!
Hurrah for me!
Lillian M. Fisher

I may have watched baseball at its best on Tv in the fall of 1988, just a few weeks before I went to be pastor of the First Baptist Church of Anchorage, Alaska, the World Series got my full attention.My underdog Los Angeles Dodgers were playing the powerful Oakland Athletics. The sports news experts wrote, " This World Series would be a no contest." One NBC commentator suggested that the Dodgers might be the worst team in history to play in the World Series.

With that, Dodger manager Tommy Lasorda, shrugged his shoulders and told his players the Bible story of David and Goliath. The first game seemed to have support for Lasorda's prophecy.

The Dodger's best hitter, outfielder Kirk Gibson was in pain from a ripped hamstring and a torn knee. He was not in the line up.

With two outs in the bottom of the ninth inning, the A's had their relief ace Dennis Eckersley on the mound holding a 4-3 lead. He walked Mike Davis, then the packed crowd erupted when they saw limping to the plate to bat, Kirk Gibson!

As I sat watching on TV this most theatrical event in baseball, my heart-beat was as if I were actually playing in the game, myself!

Pitcher Eckersley pushed the count to 3 and 2. His next pitch, a slider low and over the plate, Gibson golfed the ball and sent it into the bleachers five rows up!

I remember hollered out, "Yeah!" as if I were in the stands seeing Gibson drag his right leg circling the bases holding up both arms in triumph with his limping Hollywood "walk off" home run!

Inspired by Kirk Gibson's thrilling last pitch home run, the Dodgers went on to win the World Series 4 games to one.

This game was very personal to me because Dodger manager Tommy Lasorda was in Spring Training with me in Vero Beach, Florida when he was a pitcher for the triple A Dodger Montreal, Canada team.

When I was pastor of the large Far Hills Baptist church in Dayton, Ohio a guy came to church and said to me, "Well, Pastor Minton, you are for real."

"The other day when the Dodgers came to Cincinnati, I was invited before the game to the dugout, I asked LaSorda if he knew a Frank Minton. "Sure, he is a pastor somewhere and he has a twin brother who played too." Thanks Tommy for your confirmation.

Baseball at its best may have arrived in the person of Ohtani at 27 a Japan baseball transfer who pitches and swings the bat for the Los Angeles Angels. Already he is leading the American league in home runs and a winning pitcher. For the first time in history he is the only 2-way all-star selected for the All-Star Game. In the pregame Home Run Derby he hit one 545 foot. Lookout Babe Ruth here comes Ohtani!

It may be pure newspaper legend the way the Babe described himself, "I swing big, with everything I got. I hit big or I miss big. I like to live as big as I can!"

As I read the Bible, the apostle Peter had a similar flair. He was the home run hitter of the early church, as well as the strike out leader. When he was on, he was really on, but when he was off, he was really off.

During a terrible storm on the Sea of Galilee, the disciples found their boat in dire straits. They were frightened and felt helpless until Jesus came walking on the water. Peter said, "Tell me to come to you on the water." Jesus said, "Come ahead!" Then he stepped out of the boat with great confidence, but he began to sink and cried out, "Save me, Lord!" Immediately, Jesus reached out his hand and caught hold of him. Peter's faith at that moment was not as big as his confidence, but at least he tried! Now that was a big swing but a miss.

When people were speculating about Jesus, he asked his disciples, "Who do people say the Son of Man is?" They replied, "Some say Elijah, Jeremiah or one of the prophets. "But what about you?" he asked, "Who do you say I am?" Peter, then stepped up to the plate with the crystal truth, "You are the Son of the living God!" Jesus replied, "Blessed are you Simon, son of Jonah, for this was not revealed to you by man, but by my Father in heaven." Peter knocked the cover off the ball, this time, with an out-of-the-park home run!

When Jesus pointed out that he was going to be killed and then to rise on the third day, Peter's strong personality again came out, "Oh no, Lord! This will not happen to you!" Jesus turned and told Peter, "Get behind me, Satan! You are not thinking about God's concern." Peter didn't realize what he suggested would thwart God's plan. He thought he was being supportive of Jesus but he didn't understand the salvation plan. Jesus' primary purpose was to die on the cross, but at that moment Peter didn't know he was playing into Satan's hands. So, when he thought he was ready to swing for the fence, he was actually being called out on strikes!

Jesus was on trial, with his life on the line. Peter, the great church home run hitter, stood far off in the crowd. He was recognized by a little maid who immediately accused him of being one of the disciples, but he denied it three times by lying, "I never knew him." Just as the words came out of his mouth, Peter heard the cock crow and he remembered what Jesus had said, "This very night, before the rooster crows, you will disown me three times." He knew he had struck out, with the bases loaded. He went out and "wept bitterly."

Only by the grace of God and the forgiving love of Jesus, the game wasn't over for Peter! After Jesus arose from the dead, he entrusted Peter by saying, "Feed my sheep."

Those strike outs always haunt great home run sluggers. John Thorn and Pete Palmers, *Total baseball Encyclopedia,* gives us the facts. Babe Ruth in 2503 games hit 714 home runs and had 1330 strike outs. Hank Aaron playing in 3298 games hit 755 home runs and registered 1383 strike outs. Mickey Mantel who could hit the ball further than any baseball player in history slammed 536 home runs but struck out an amazing 1710 times!

Dan Liberthson in his book, *The Pitch is on the Way: Poems About Baseball and Life,* gives us a great feel of home runs and strike outs.

> There's nothing left to do
> but swing and go for broke.
> I may come out a hero,
> I may end up a goat.

I didn't like getting embarrassed." Lance Berkman of the Houston Astros normally a 300+ hitter was quoted in the *Houston Chronicle* April 27, 2009 after going 0 for 16 before getting his first hit of the season to put his club ahead of the Cincinnati Reds, "It's like having three strikes against you, with no chance to win. There you stand soldiering your bat on your shoulder after three pitches, all called strikes. It's a very depressing moment." Lance knows well that the worst feeling for a hitter is to be called out on strikes.

Let me tell you something, son,
Before you get much older,
You cannot hit the ball, my friend,
With your bat on your shoulder.
Bill Bryon
"The singing umpire"

My twin, Fred, played three years in the minors for the Dodgers and the Orioles; he was never a home run hitter, but didn't strike out much, either. His baseball philosophy was: "The two most dramatic plays in baseball are home runs and strike outs and I'm looking for all the plays in between."

Henry Chadwick, a sports writer who started covering baseball in 1858 for *The New York Clipper,* invented the baseball box score and the famous "K" for strike outs in 1861. He chose the strong letter k from the word strike and some feel his last name ending with a "k" was another factor in his choice. To this very day fans bring homemade "K" signs to the stadium and tape them to the walls or the facade of upper seating levels, to indicate the number of strike outs their hometown pitcher is producing. The backward "K" indicates a called third strike. This is a real boost for a pitcher because strike outs are to a pitcher what home runs are to a batter.

Even though baseball is a team sport it becomes a one on one pitcher and hitter contest at every "batter up" situation. Today 2021, there is a real concern that for the last twelve consecutive years strikeouts have exceeded hits drastically. The concern is that baseball may become less exciting. That is the reason pitchers are searched to find if any substances on their glove or clothing that could be placed on the ball to give an unfair spinning advantage.

The internet site, *Exploration,* gives a most unusual story about two of the most interesting Ks in baseball history. On April 2, 1931, the New York Yankees stopped in Chattanooga, Tennessee, for an exhibition game on their way home from spring training. A crowd of 4,000 came to watch, including scores of reporters, wire services and even a newsreel camera. Jackie Mitchell came in to relieve with only one good pitch, a wicked dropping curve ball. The first batter Jackie faced was Babe Ruth. Ruth took ball one, and then swung and missed the next two pitches. The pitcher's fourth pitch caught the corner of the plate and the umpire called it a strike. Struck out, Ruth kicked the dirt and stomped to the Yank's dugout.

The next batter was Lou Gehrig. He stepped to the plate and swung at the first sinker. Strike one! He swung twice more, hitting nothing but air. Mitchell had fanned the Sultan of Swat and the Iron Horse, back to back. Amazing, you must agree, but even more incredible, is the fact that Jackie Mitchell was a seventeen year old girl!

Babe Ruth's final farewell was broadcast coast to coast on April 27, 1947, when he appeared at the twenty-fifth anniversary celebration of Yankee Stadium. Ruth, his body wracked by throat cancer, used a bat for a cane as he walked to the microphone at home plate. They said he looked and sounded like a condemned man, even though he was only fifty-three years old. He would be dead in two months.

Fred and I were playing catch in the front yard when mother called, "Come inside to hear the last words of the greatest baseball player in the world." Our only radio was a small brown plastic Philco, on top of our white refrigerator in the kitchen. We were twelve at the time, just beginning to play the game and soaking up everything that was related to baseball.

The Great Bambino spoke in a low, guttural, raspy voice that we strained to hear. It was a rather short speech, "You know, this baseball game of ours, comes up from the youth. That means the boys. And after you have been a boy and grow up and know how to play ball, then you come to the boys you see representing themselves today in our national pastime." His talk was soon forgotten by us, but it made a lasting impression that even the great ones were subject to disease and death.

I am grateful, as a boy, I did not know of his personal life of debauchery and immorality. If only his life off the field could have been as remarkable as his ball playing, just think what a wonderful influence he could have been.

Lou Gehrig was the good guy hero and his number 4 shirt (batted 4 in batting line up) was only overshadowed by number 3 Babe Ruth. The press adored "the Bambinos" flamboyant personality and outlandish ways. Even though both men batted 3 and 4 in the batting line up the true quiet star was the "iron horse" Gehrig.

As he faced death learning he had the incurable disease Amyotrophic lateral sclerosis (which now bears his name) on July 4, 1939 at Yankee Stadium, After receiving a bear hug from Babe Ruth he announced"...I consider myself the luckiest man on the face of the earth." Two years later he died at age 36. Only a God loving man could make such a statement!

I praise God for the good life of the "Babe Ruth" of our present day, St. Louis' first baseman, Albert Pujols. In 2008, he won the Roberto Clemente Award, which is given to the major league player who "best exemplifies the game of baseball." Pujols, who is a two time National League MVP winner, stated to *Sports Illustrated* magazine, "The award is the most meaningful award I have ever won."

It's wonderful there are ball players like Dodgers pitcher, Orel Hershiser, who among many honors and awards, has been named MVP, Sportsman of the Year, Major League Player of the Year and the Cy Young Award. In 1988, he broke the "unbreakable" record of pitching fifty-nine scoreless innings. But a year later Orel's career was about to end, having to undergo radical shoulder reconstructive surgery. Yet he depended upon the Lord, "Commit your way to the Lord; and trust Him," continues to be one of his bedrock Bible scriptures. His personal testimony is stirring as printed in the magazine, *Focus on the Family*, July 2002, "Late one night I pulled the Gideon Bible from my night stand at the Buckaroo Motel in Scottsdale, Arizona and read from the book of John. I slipped to my knees next to the bed. Openly, I confessed my sins; I invited Jesus Christ into my life and received Him as my Savior by faith."

When I was in New York this year I went to Brooklyn. There, at Cypress Hills Cemetery, not far from where Ebbets Field once stood, is the grave marker of Jackie Robinson, the historic first black major leaguer. The inscription is profound, "A life is not important except in the impact it has on other lives."

When a player hits one out of the park, fans feel they have hit one too. The home run has become the extra ingredient that makes baseball a "now excitement," whether the home town team is winning, or not. As prolific writer, Leonard Koppett, so apply stated, "A home run is a home run - win or lose. The non-homer psychology will never return. For the home run can change a game immediately and turn the whole game around. The home run is the ingredient that spices up the game. The central figure in baseball was once the pitcher, but now it's the home run hitter. The home run gives instant gratification and the fans love it!" It has been estimated that more than 200,000 Major League home runs have been hit since the big leagues were established. That's amazing!

I hit only one home run in my professional career, but what a sensational feeling! Since I was a pitcher, I was not expected to do much with the bat, but there was that desire to "knock one outt'a the park." I remember it as well as if it were yesterday. I was pitching for the Dodgers' farm team in the old Sooner State League with the Shawnee, Oklahoma club. We were playing against a New York Yankees farm team from McAlester, Oklahoma. As I came to the plate, the Yankees were ahead 2-0. The pitch came singing in and before I realized it, my bat had connected. The ball went booming its way over the scoreboard! It was a dinger! I was the most surprised guy on the diamond as I jogged around the base paths.

To add to the excitement of the night, my twin brother Fred, who was playing centerfield and batting in the number two slot, came up in the same inning. Gene Wallace our shortstop, who had worked a walk, was on first base. "Hit one, like your twin brother" came the cries from the crowd in the stands. It really put Fred under pressure, but he was man for the task. As if it was a dream come true, Fred hit one in almost the identical spot, over the scoreboard. That day we became the "dynamic duo." Our teammates pointed out to us the next week that we made print in *Sporting News,* the baseball magazine. It was in small print, "Identical twins hit identical home runs."

The desire to hit a home run is the ultimate goal for a batter. Who, as a little leaguer, has not in his mind trotted around Yankee Stadium as a second Babe Ruth. The spirit of going the "full yard" and coming home a winner, grips all of us.

Roger Granet's poem gives us a good glimpse of that desire in the mind of a child.

Boyhood Baseball

At bat, in bed, beneath the
Sandlot sky, I would be
Anyone I could imagine
In pinstripes, not pajamas.
Roger Granet

The twelve who followed Jesus also had that home run blood coursing through their veins. "Who is the greatest in the Kingdom of Heaven?" was the question that got their interest. You see, when Jesus was not with them, they began to argue about it. James and John, with encouragement from their mother, were right in the middle of the mix.

It's sad, but the chosen twelve were not above that hero desire. Amazingly, they had the problem in a big way! What might have begun with small words of pride by James and John, soon became a full-blown dispute among them.

Jesus never intended for his followers to have a special ranking among themselves. He did not want his "Church" to get jealous over who was considered his closest friends. Jesus wanted them to be together as a team to do his work on earth. He didn't want a "Gospel Hall of Fame."

When they arrived at the town of Capernaum, Jesus looked intently at his disciples for he knew their hearts. They could not cover up the argument they had among themselves about who was the greatest. "What were you arguing about on the road?" The disciples were stunned by the question and stood before their master in silence. Jesus sat down and said to them, "Whoever wants to be first must place himself last of all and be the servant of all."

"And he took a child and set him in the midst of them. I tell you the truth, unless you change and become like little children, you will never enter the kingdom of heaven. Therefore, whoever humbles himself like this child, is the greatest in the kingdom of heaven."

When following Jesus, there is no place for self pride or jealousy. The ground is strangely level at the foot of the Cross. In baseball jargon,

Jesus was saying, "You don't have to be a home run slugger to be placed in my batting order. You don't need to 'knock it out of the park' to play on my team. Just trust and follow me!"

A Major League baseball season has a 162 game schedule. No other sport has the luxury of so many games. Chuck Tanner, long time Major League manager, 1970 - 1988, is quoted in Poland's inspirational book, *Steal Away,* "What you have to remember is that baseball isn't a week or a month but a season—and a season is a long time."

Consistency becomes the hallmark for a player to stay in the majors. Hank Aaron earned the nickname of "Mr. Consistency" for his steady homerun production every season. Torii Hunter, former centerfielder for the Los Angeles Angels, is not a household baseball name and he may never be in the Hall of Fame, but he played day in and day out with such excellence that he had a position in center field waiting for him every season. In fact, his fielding in the outfield was as consistent as his hitting. He won the Gold Glove Award every year for a decade.

Every day is preparation for the next game. You don't have time to "lick your wounds" over a strike out or a ball that got away from you. Your great opportunity is the next game. So the daily routine is a must. Take your cuts at batting practice. Run your laps faithfully with full vigor. Get a good nights rest. Stay away from the parties. Work out to keep in shape. Eat good wholesome foods. Keep focused. Don't live like the Prodigal Son!

On road trips, several of us packed our Bibles, because we realized to consistently follow Jesus is to read his Word. Every day, read the Bible with thought. Pray from your heart. Share your faith with others. You will, day by day grow in grace. You don't need to force it, to be spiritual. Just be consistent. When we over-swing spiritually, trying to do the big holy thing, such as being critical of others or having a "holier than thou" attitude, we often find ourselves with a big K.

My high school baseball coach Monk Edwards, would holler out, "Not a hard hit Emery, just a sweet one. Swing easy and let your power do the work."

Gene Wallace, former coach at Oklahoma Baptist University, was a skinny shortstop when he broke into the minors with the Dodgers at Shawnee, Oklahoma. He was so frail he didn't look like he could ever be a power hitter. Game after game, he took his regular cuts at the plate;

his batting average was good but nothing sensational. Then it happened! Gene hit one out of the park. We were amazed!

"Man, how did you do that?" we asked as we celebrated in the dugout. The surprised Wallace just shrugged and said, "Nothing more than I always do. I just swung the best I could" Our manger Jack Banta, reinforced Gene's discovery. "Just keep going to the plate, swing at the ball the best you know how and you'll get your home runs." And did Gene ever collect home runs that season! The next year Wallace's contract jumped from the lowly class D Shawnee club, to the mighty Triple - A Montreal team, simply because he was consistent at the bat. Each time he came to bat, he was determined to do his best, nothing more, nothing less.

Jesus said, "Take up your cross daily and follow me," nothing more and nothing less.

"Take up thy cross and follow Me," I heard my Master say;
"I gave My life to ransom thee, Surrender your all today."
Wherever He leads I'll go, Wherever He leads I'll go,
I'll follow my Christ who loves me so, Wherever He leads I'll go.
Falls Creek
B.B. McKinney, 1936

CHAPTER 10

GIVE YOURSELF UP

You hold the bat at eye-level,
knees bent, get down to meet the ball,
preparing to give yourself up
for the common good.
Lucky Jacobs

"I lay down my life for the sheep."
Jesus

BASEBALL IS A team game. A winning team cannot rely solely on a few long ball hitters or a couple of good pitchers. It takes some good, well placed short hits as well. That's where a bunt comes into play. As George F. Will, writes in his book, *Bunts*, "Bunts are modest and often useful things, although they are not always well understood." It takes nine players working together to win a game and that means bunts are part of the batting scheme for every player.

You won't find Phil Rizzuto, Hall of Fame short stop for the Yankees, in the books as a great slugger. Yet, he did all the little things, bunt, hit behind the runner, defensive fielding gems; things you need to win games.

Martin Luther King Jr., known the world over, a giant among men, was basically a humble Baptist preacher. He was thrust to become the leader in the Civil rights Movement. He's words are monumental, "If I cannot do great things, I can do small things in a great way."

Today, the bunt is known as a "sacrifice bunt" but in the 1880's to the early 1900's it was a huge weapon in pro baseball. Team strategy was to play for one run at a time. Ball games of the early 1900s were sloppy and amateurish compared to today's play but the players did their best to make it a game of precision. The bunt played right into this strategy.

Bunting and base stealing were the primary weapons of the day, for the ball was so dead hardly anyone could slug it into the stands. The balls were much softer than they are today. The inside stuffing was usually rubber cuttings wrapped with yarn, then covered with horsehide. In fact, the ball was so light it could not be thrown more than two hundred feet. Of course, since 1927 all of that has changed.

Baseball by the Rules, states that the balls are the same size (9 to 91/2 inches) and weigh the same (between 5 and 5 1/4 ounces). The present specs for weight and circumference were established in 1872. The process of replacing the rubber center with cork and the improved machine tightening of the 330 yards of yarn, has made for the lively ball. It's what's on the inside that counts. There are two other changes, which perhaps, do not play a significant role in the liveliness of the ball. The horsehide covering of the ball has been replaced with cowhide. The other factor is that a clean ball is to be kept in play during the game. As it was in the early days of baseball, each ball must have 108 red stitches, which are now machine sewn. According to the April 2010 issue of *Spirit Magazine,* the Rawlings company of St. Louis, Missouri manufactures over two million baseballs a year.

The new white baseballs are shiny and slick, so mud is hand-rubbed on them. This mud has been helping pitchers get a grip on the ball for seventy years. Incredibly, there is a special mud for major league play. It comes from feldspar-rich clay from two secret holes in a New Jersey swamp land according to *National Geographic Magazine.* But in the minors, the umpires many times have to find their own source of mud.

It is interesting to note, in early baseball the home run was considered a novelty item. Some people complained that a home run would end a rally, which could have lasted on and on. The lowly bunt was in and the home run was out!

John Thorn in, *Total Baseball,* gives us an account that shows the seriousness of the bunt in baseball. "Red Murray, an outfielder with the New York Giants in 1910, stepped to the plate in the ninth inning of a tie game with Pittsburg. With a man on second and no outs, manager John McGraw followed orthodox strategy and signaled Murray to lay one down the third base line. However, Pirate pitcher Howie Camnitz smelled the call and threw his pitch high and tight. But that was in Murrays's alley. He swung away and sent the ball over the left-field fence to win the game.

Murray whistled his way around the bases and into the shower. But he changed his tune when McGraw found him in the club house and fined him twenty-five dollars for disregarding a sign." That was a hefty fine in those days.

Bunting is still an essential part of any team's strategy but sluggers don't like to lose a chance to hit the ball for a round tripper. Baseball historian, John Thorn, gives us another inside account that bears this out. "One afternoon the Brooklyn star, Babe Herman was up next to go to the plate with a man on first and no one out. Dodger manager, Wilbur Robinson, called for the bunt. Babe chuckled and then muttered to the bat boy who was nearby, 'If Robbie thinks I'm gonna' bunt, he's crazy. Watch this!'

Herman purposely bunted the first two pitches foul, then drove the third over the right field wall. As Herman rounded the bases, Robinson shook his head and grunted, 'I shoulda' known that the Babe can't bunt'."

To give yourself up and lay down a sacrifice, is difficult for any hitter to do. When I pitched, I loved to take my swings at the plate. Usually, my task at bat was to bunt a runner to the next base. In close games, managers don't want pitchers on the base paths because, it tires their legs and affects their pitching.

During a close game in the California State League, it was my time to bat with no one on base. Ray "Little Buffalo" Perry, our manager said, "O.K., Minton get up there and strike out. Don't even take the bat off your shoulder. I don't want you running around those bases."

"Aw, Ray," I protested, "Can I just swing at one?"

"OK, but you had better hit it out of here" were his relenting remarks.

A big juicy fast ball came booming across the plate and I swung with all my might. Bingo, I not only connected, but the ball went flying out to center field, looking like a sure home run. But as I ran toward first base, I saw the ball hit the fence, so I had to hustle around second and on to third, where I slid in with a triple!

"Now you've done it!" exclaimed "Little Buffalo," who was coaching third base. "Minton, you're through! Scott Breeden, warm up!"

That year, 1957, Fran Bonair was our left fielder and a prolific hitter. In fact, he led the entire professional baseball world with a staggering batting average of .436. Every pitcher he faced had his work cut out.

Toward the end of the season, the outcome of every game weighed heavily on the pennant race. In the ninth inning of a crucial game, we were one run behind the Giant's Bakersfield, California club. With two men on base and two outs, we had the good fortune of Bonair coming to the plate. Everyone in our home stands was alive with anticipation. We knew, with one swing of the bat the game would be over.

With mighty Bonair taking his cuts at the plate, it was going to be good. Stepping into the box, Fran glanced down at third to get the sign from our manager. But, he could hardly believe his eyes. Perry, of all things, had given the bunt signal! "Little Buffalo" had noticed the Bakersfield third baseman was playing far back, almost on the outfield grass, anticipating a hard smash from Bonair.

Puzzled, Bonair stepped out of the batter's box and looked again, to be sure he had caught the right sign. Sure enough, there it was. Perry, again, went through the three motions: touching the front of his shirt, the hand clap and then the bunt signal, right hand to his chin (skin on skin). "Me bunt? I can't believe it!" were the thoughts of our great slugger. Reluctantly, he stepped back into the box to face the pitcher. To the complete surprise of the Bakersfield club, Bonair laid down a beautiful bunt along the third base line. Our runner on third, Charlie Smith, scored and Doug Camilli on second took off for third. The opposing team was so shaken by the unexpected play, that their catcher, who had taken a throw from the third baseman, threw the ball into left field in his attempt to throw Camilli out at third. Camilli then sped home with the winning run. We had a "walk off" bunt for the win!

Fran Bonair, the power hitter of the 1957 season, won the game with his little "baby hit." He was willing to forget his hitter's pride and sacrifice himself.

Everyone is trying to accomplish something big,
Not realizing life is made up of little things.
Ken Vanway

This is graphically illustrated by an account in Luke's gospel. "As he looked up, Jesus saw the rich putting their gifts into the temple treasury. He also saw a poor widow put in two very small copper coins. 'I tell you the truth,' he said, 'this poor widow has put in more than all the others. All these people gave their gifts out of their wealth, but she, out of her poverty, put all she had to live on'." A sacrifice is never overlooked by God.

Jesus could have come to this earth in his heavenly glory, but he chose to be born in a manger. Even though Jesus possessed, "All power in heaven and on earth," he humbled himself to become one of us. He came to share life with us from a simple carpenter's home. He walked among the common people, doing his ministry of healing the sick and having concern for the rich and poor alike.

He didn't parade as a mighty conqueror on a charging white horse, but in humility rode on a donkey's back as he entered Jerusalem. This also gave evidence that Jesus was the Messiah predicted by the prophets. He steadfastly lived a humble perfect life, to go to the Cross. His power was exerted when He arose from the grave to overcome sin, death and hell. He was the perfect sacrifice of all for us. Jesus said, "a reason for many that they may have life everlasting."

In 1948, when Fred and I were fourteen, we wanted to help some neighborhood boys get a baseball team together. They wanted to play in the eleven and twelve-year aged bracket of the American Legion League. Since a lot of our players were from disadvantaged homes, playing on a baseball team would give them a sense of accomplishment and something to enjoy. They were not quite street kids, but our best pitcher did spend some months in a reform school.

Searching around, we found the Wichita North End Kiwanis Club might be interested in sponsoring a team for boys. This meant uniforms and equipment were to be furnished by their club. The Kiwanians, agreed to sponsor our boys team on the condition that Fred and I would be the managers and take full responsibility of the team. Since the North End was basically blue collar, the men were tied to their jobs; none of them could get off work in the mornings, when the games were played. With a shoestring budget, the treasurer for the Kiwanis Club, bought marked-down black uniforms. The gold lettering was a gift of the store owner. Our need to transport the team was solved when a member of the club and owner of the Cochran Funeral Home, furnished our team with a black hearse and driver.

It was some sight to see that hearse arriving at a ball diamond, loaded with our baseball team and equipment. Our boys would pile out, wearing their black wool uniforms, trimmed in gold, with matching stockings and gold baseball caps. It was quite amusing! There was no question, the North End guys had arrived!

We figured kids their age couldn't field or throw very well, so we taught our boys how to bunt. "You hold the bat with both hands, one behind the fat part and the other at the bottom of the handle. Move the bat around like the rudder of a boat. Whatever direction you want the ball to go, point the heavy end of the bat that way. Don't strike or lunge at the ball. Imagine your bat as a glove and catch the ball with it; then run like crazy!"

We practiced and practiced; they learned to bunt and run! Every game was bunt and run. Fred and I were right; they couldn't field and throw those balls that had been bunted. Throughout the games, we occasionally had our boys swing away. This kept the opposing teams' infielders from moving in close to field the bunts. This greatly frustrated the other teams, especially the adult coaches. Game after game, this strategy made our boys winners! Our team won the league, which put us in the championship play-off.

The championship game put some fear and anxiety in the minds of our players. For the first time they were playing under the lights in a small stadium. It was big time, but our boys were scrappers. The opposing team, the Braves, looked sharp in their white uniforms with red trim, matching red stockings and white hats with red trim. Our black uniforms were quite a contrast.

Before the game, we huddled our team together, gave them our brief instruction to lay down those bunts and run! We had told them throughout the season, a bunt was like David with a sling shot facing Goliath with his armor and sword. We prayed for a good game and, as they took to the field, we hollered, "Remember David and be sure to touch all the bases!"

You can't believe how well our boys bunted, ran and stole those bases! The white suited Braves fumbled those little bunts and threw the ball all over the diamond! Our boys touched all the bases and the Braves never came close to catching us! The delinquent pitcher didn't want to bunt, his second time at bat. Since we had two of our bunters on first and second, I said, "OK, swing away." With new found freedom, he knocked the ball over the centerfield fence! After the big win, the trophy was celebrated by all of our players in front of the stands. Then we happily trooped back to our waiting black hearse.

A few weeks later our team was feted with a celebration banquet by the businessmen of the Club. The trophy was then presented to the North End Wichita Kiwanis Club in appreciation of their sponsorship. A reporter from, *The Wichita North End Newspaper,* took pictures and put an article about the event on the front page.

When Jesus spoke, he showed people how to celebrate life with everyday small things. He talked about the obvious: water, bread, light, flowers, sparrows, trees, salt and seeds. He talked of going the second mile, giving away your coat and sharing a cup of cold water. These were little things and yet they were big. Jesus said, "I tell you the truth, whatever you did for one of the least of these brothers of mine, you did for me."

Jesus performed many miracles in his three year ministry. He healed a man born blind, he calmed a storm on the Sea of Galilee, and he fed five thousand at one time, all by his miraculous power. Jesus did these things because, "I must be about my Father's business." It was not to impress as a "grand stander" miracle worker but to show that He was the one and only true Son of God. "See that no one misleads you. For many will come in my name saying, 'I am the Christ, and will mislead many'." Every miracle he performed was also out of love and compassion extending the Kingdom of God in the hearts of the people.

Jesus did not speak with intellectual snobbery or overpowering rhetoric. When he spoke, it was with words the common people totally understood. Baseball's play-by-play announcers speak the language of the average fan. Their colorful words spike up the interest and excitement of the game. Hall of Fame pitcher Dizzy Dean, was loved by fans all over America for his down to earth jargon, as he announced games over the radio in the forties. School teachers though, raised more than a little ruckus with his slaughter of the King's English. Dizzy countered with, "Let the teachers teach English and I will teach baseball. There is a lot of people in the United States who say isn't, and they ain't eating." His hallmark quip was, "He slud into third."

Baseball puts spice and vinegar and sometimes in boisterous terms but it keeps the game from sounding dull and boring. In fact, words of the game have filtered its way far beyond the diamond into the everyday language of life such as "How are things going?" well, it's like "no runs, no hits, no errors" meaning a slow day; or "how did you do?" "I struck out" when the result came in. The country is as American as baseball

In like term words from the Bible has its impact in everyday life when safe in a car accident "saved by God's grace," or when describing helping someone's problem, "I had to go that extra mile."

The more you love Baseball the more its vernacular becomes part of speech without realizing it. Baseball becomes more than runs, hits and errors or statistical terms. It becomes a heartbeat of life.

The Bible has even a greater part of a Christian life. Its more than a study of words. Jesus said, "follow me" in word and deed. "You are the light and salt of the world". Words of action with vitality. It's more than saying the right words. Its being in love with God through trust by living, walking and worshiping Jesus.

Jesus continued to bring revolutionary ideas: "Do unto others as you would have them do to you, love your enemies, do good to them who hurt you and stop worrying and trust your heavenly Father." In baseball jargon he was saying, Lay a bunt down, and don't be afraid to sacrifice yourself to get the runner over. Little sacrificial bunts have big dividends!

> "It seems that no one appreciates a sacrifice
> except in baseball and the Bible."
> **Anonymous**

> Little drops of water
> Little grains of sand
> Fill the mighty ocean
> And make the mighty land.
>
> Little acts of kindness,
> Little things you do,
> Makes me so in love with you.
> **Julia Carney, 1845**

When I was pastor of the First Baptist Church of Anchorage, Alaska, I became more aware of the grandeur of the world God has created for us. It was awe inspiring to drive along the road to the ski resort, Alyeska on the rim of the Pacific Ocean, where the Japanese current brings the Beluga whales. As we drove we could look up and see white Dall sheep scampering along the rocky ledges. It was breathtaking to see the gorgeous snow covered Chugach Mountains, which humble Anchorage's skyline. It was awesome to know that the snow covered glaciers, were made of snowflakes that fell from the heavens two thousand years ago, when Jesus walked the earth. The amazing ice fog floating in the frigid sunlight and the Aurora Borealis drifting in the cold night sky, gave an otherworldly feeling. With all this mystique of winter came the anticipated return of spring and summer with flowers exploding in brilliant colors of red, yellow and purple.

In the midst of this creation, God has allowed us to have baseball under the midnight sun in Fairbanks, Alaska. On the longest day of the year, June 21st, the Alaskan Goldpanners, a semi-pro team made up of good college players, have a game. It begins on the summer solstice at 10:30 p.m. without lights, continuing through the hour of midnight and often lasts as late as 2 a.m.

Dan Schlossberg in his book, *Baseball Bits,* writes, "The game is so popular, outstanding major leaguers, Tom Seaver, Dave Winfield and Barry Bonds all personally paid their way to play."

Bobby Doer, outstanding second baseman for the Boston Red Sox, when I was a teenager, rates the thrill of playing this midnight game, right up there with the World Series and the Hall of Fame games.

God created this wonderful universe for us to enjoy. "In the Beginning, God created the heavens and the earth." His creation makes me love Him all the more.

According to the devotional book, *The One Year Book of Hymns,* Maltbie Babcock was an outstanding baseball pitcher for Syracuse University and kept himself in shape by running. While pastor of the First Presbyterian church in Lockport, New York he ran in the morning to the brow of the hill two miles away and looked over Lake Ontario. Before he left his study to run, he would tell his church staff, "I am going out to see my Father's world." This inspired him to write the most unforgettable hymn extolling God's handiwork in nature.

This Is My Father's World

This is my Father's world,
And to my listening ears
All nature sings, and round me rings
The music of the spheres.

This is my Father's world;
I rest me in the thought
Of rocks and trees, of skies and seas –
His hand the wonders wrought.

This is my Father's world,
The birds their carol's raise,
The morning light, the lily white,
Declare their Maker's praise.

This is my Father's world:
He shines in all that's fair;
In the rustling grass I hear him pass,
He speaks to me everywhere.

This is my Father's world,
O let me ne'er forget
That though the wrong seems oft so strong,
God is the ruler yet.

This is my Father's world:
The battle is not done;
Jesus, who died shall be satisfied,
And earth and heav'n be one.
Maltbie Davenport Babcock (1858-1901)

CHAPTER 11

THAT'S THE WAY THE BALL BOUNCES

So many ways to err
on so many days and nights!
it's amazing anyone
gets anything right.
Dan Liberthson

ERRORS WERE COMMON in early baseball because players did not wear gloves. This seems incredible! Today, they are so elementary, we don't give it a thought, since gloves are the primary tools for catching the ball. However, for the first twenty years, baseball was played without gloves. The way they played the ball was, to knock it down with their hands, pick it up and then throw it. In those early days, hand protection was viewed as a sign of weakness and only sissies used them. The pain of the sport was to be endured without complaint. Fortunately, the ball was not as compact as it is today, so it was not as hard.

As baseball grew, so did the use of gloves. It wasn't until 1871, that a strip of leather wrapped around the injured hand of catcher, Doug Allison, became the first baseball glove. Then it took five more years, before another player, Charles Waitt, first baseman for St. Louis, placed a flesh colored leather strip glove on his hand. Soon after, gloves became accepted when star first baseman, Albert Spalding began using one. He later founded the great Spalding Company that makes sporting equipment. By the mid 1890's, it became the norm to play with a glove.

As improvement in the construction of gloves came about, the players fielding improved immensely. These gloves brought about a sharp decline in both runs and errors. According to, *"Fascinating*

Baseball Fact," "The Pittsburg Pirates made over 300 errors in 1916." Compare that to less than 100 errors committed by the average Major League team each year.

Baseball failure is a norm: the acceptance of defeat. The best teams lose one out of every three games and the finest hitters fail seven times out of ten. Baseball is a discouraging game! The greatest baseball saga in poetry, "Casey at the bat," ends in utter despair. "There is no joy in Mudville, for mighty Casey had struck out."

After a Casey type loss, the disappointed fan shrugs his shoulders and murmurs, "Well, that's the breaks of the game," as he forsakes the stadium, only to trudge back the next game day. The acceptance of defeat is a common malady. Trying to measure up to a perfect standard and mostly missing the mark, is what makes emotions rise and fall during each game. At times, it's easy to get a certain "down" feeling.

After you strike out,
Ground out, pop up,
make errors, lose games,
and deal with bad calls,
The rest of life is easy.
Poem search.com

The Bible tells us, even the Apostle Paul had those kinds of days. "Oh, wretched man that I am. The things I want to do, I find myself not doing and the things I don't want to do, I find myself doing. How can I escape this dilemma?" That's when he gets focused again and bursts out saying, "But thanks be to God, who gives us the victory in Christ Jesus!"

I remember, during my pitching days, if I threw a wild pitch, I'd say, "This just can't be me!" I caught myself thinking, "Well, I must not be much of a pitcher, anyway." But, I'd get focused again and concentrate on the next pitch, so my mind could control my arm. I had to realize that it wasn't perfection that I was after, but the best performance I could muster. This attitude was secret of my success.

In a Peanuts cartoon by Charles M Schultz, Charlie Brown is pitching in a baseball game. He throws to the hitter at home plate and "pow" the ball is hit so hard that it knocks Charlie Brown right off the pitching mound causing him to be in the air upside down!

Falling back on the ground Charlie Brown says to himself, "Every now and then I become plagued by self-doubts.

Hitting a pitched ball is the most difficult thing to do in all of sports. A batter has only a fraction of a second to determine whether to hit a ninety mile an hour fast ball or let it go. The average hitter (.250) is a struggling batter. But all good hitters (.300) know that it never gets easier. I learned as a kid, baseball was one of the hardest sports to play. You have a round bat and a round ball which you try to hit squarely.

In another Peanuts cartoon by Schultz; Charlie Brown and Lucy are trying to play baseball.

"Lucy that's the fifth time you've struck out! You're swinging too hard, all you have to do is meet the ball!"

Lucy retorted, "that's what I tried to do, my bat was there, but the ball didn't show up!"

Baseball is a game of numbers. It places a precise measure on a player's ability. Just saying, "He's a pretty good hitter," is not enough to tell a real fan what kind of hitter he is. The fan has to know if he bats .260 or .315. Then, with that detailed description, he can size up the player. Success or failure cannot be hidden. The numbers show it all, for they are right in front of you on the stadium's big screen.

The Bible is that way, for it tells the truth. Even though King David, "was a man after God's own heart," he committed adultery with his secret lover, Bathsheba. She became pregnant, so David had her husband, Uriah, killed in battle. Then he married her to cover his sins.

The Bible tells how he was exposed by the prophet, Nathan. God's prophet stood face to face with David and told him a story about a powerful man, taking advantage of a weaker man. King David reacted with anger toward the one who took advantage and demanded, "Who is this man?" Nathan replied, "You are the man!"

David with sadness prays to God in Psalm 51, "Restore to me the joy of your Salvation"

Last Sunday in Church I heard a new song that touched my heart, "Our sins they are many, His mercy is more". Amen and amen!

Down in the lower minors, the field of play was not always in the best shape. Sometimes, clods of dirt or small pebbles in the path of the ball, made it take an unexpected bounce and cause an error. We often shrugged ours shoulders and acknowledged, "That's the way the ball bounces." Sometimes, when a hapless infielder had a difficult time with an extra crazy bouncing ball we would yell, from the dugout, "It's alive! Get a stick and kill it!"

The Apostle Paul had some of those bounces, that he couldn't quite handle. But he didn't let those errors stop him. "But, one thing I do: Forgetting what is behind and straining toward what is ahead, I press on toward the goal, to win the prize for which God has called me heavenward, in Christ Jesus."

A comedy of errors was related by baseball historian, John Thorn, in his colossal reference book, *Total Baseball,* about a play in the 1970 World Series game between the American League, Baltimore Orioles and the National League, Cincinnati Reds. "The Reds player Carbo, slid home, but he never touched the plate. The Orioles Catcher Hendrick, made the tag with his glove, but had the ball in his other hand. Burkett, the umpire, was caught in the three-way collision with the catcher and the runner. The impact caused him to be flung into the air. He landed with his right thumb extended up, meaning that the runner was out. In reality, the spill had so turned him around that he was facing the outfield and not home plate. Thus he could not possibly have seen the play! All three made errors! When the ruling was made, the Reds player, Carbo, was called out. The next day, photos in the newspaper showed what had actually occurred in the bizarre play." If we'd had instant replay in 1970, there's no telling what the call would have been.

The Error of their Ways

Trying too hard, that's error:
   fireballer over-throws,
   lurches off the mound
as his pitch runs to the backstop.

Not trying hard enough, that's error:
   catcher backhands a snake pitch
instead of jumping for the body block.

Feeling too much pain, that's error:
aging first-baseman waves
a slow roller between his legs
past his knees' helpless shouts.

Haste (making waste), that's error:
second baseman turns his shortstop's throw
before he finds the seams; first sacker,
at the top of his leap, sees it sail away.

Taking what's not yours, that's error:
third baseman flubs a shallow fly
by rights his left fielder's; then the rattled
rookie pitcher gophers a homerun ball.

Distraction, that's error:
bouncer kisses the shortstop's glove heel,
broken bat barrel flipping toward him;
E6, undeserved, but so it stays.

Dreaming, that's error:
left fielder gets a late start—
rising liner ticks his web
for double trouble.

Overconfidence, that's error:
center fielder lazily one-hands
the high fly ball that finds
a nonexistent hole in his glove.

Misjudgement, that's error:
right fielder overthrows his cut-off man
and suddenly the runner stands
safe at third, smiling.

So many ways to err
on so many days and nights!
it's amazing anyone
gets anything right.
Dan Liberthson

Matthew Futterman in the April 2010, *Wall Street Journal,* writes, "Some of the most innovative franchises have decided to rebuild their lineups around the philosophy—that defense is the key to victory. All over baseball, teams are being remade along these lines."

Major league Baseball wants to see more offense as pitching has become the dominant factor in Baseball. In 2019, the last full season of record, strikouts have increased for 12 consecutive years up 33 percent from the seasons back to 2007. In each of the last three seasons strickouts have exceeded hits. This has brought a big time concern for MLB executives. By the middle of May 2021 already 6 no hitters; the record for the whole season is 7.

The play of baseball has changed from bunts in the years up to the 1920's to the homerun barrages, now in 2000's the pitching demands center stage. There are many factors involved in these changes. Basically it's the size and prowess the pitchers who throw at an average of 92 miles per hour and stand in height of six feet five inches.

In the days I pitched the sports writers called me a tall rangey pitcher at 6 feet! Today I couldn't make the line-up.

Pitcher's know they don't get no-hitters or wins by themselves. In every no hitter or great win, terrific defensive fielding gems are made. After Matt Garza pitched a no hitter for Tampa Bay, he was quoted by Fred Goodall, AP baseball writer, "The defense made great plays. I really can't say enough about them." His wife Serina, sent this I phone message: "I wish – I – there- , with tears,"

Likewise the pastor can't do it all in the work of the Kingdom of God. As God blessed me with wonderful growing much alive churches, I know it was not just my preaching alone. Infact, I preached on Sunday and my people preached every day in their daily lives.

Measuring a player's worth by defense, instead of power hitting, is the reason the Gold Glove Award is presented every year for excellence in fielding. Since 1957, the Rawlings Gold Glove Award has been given to Major League players to commemorate the best fielding performance, at each position in the American and National Leagues.

A little nine year boy excitedly runs into his house "I got a hit, I got a hit! But the ball was caught before it hit the ground!"

The Outfielder

Batter's up
Not a sound,
Glove to the ground
Face to crowd.
Rebecca Kai Dotlich

Dr. Nancy D. Becker, retired pastor of the Ogden Dunes Community Church, in Portage, Indiana, has written a terrific analogy about baseball errors and life. She has so aptly used her theology and baseball sense to show the dilemma of the human predicament, of trying to measure up to a standard of perfection, but always failing. She received her baseball love from her father who was a rabid Tiger fan. Dr. Becker said, "There is something about baseball that gets into one's blood."

She illustrates our problem with the truth in the Bible, "All have sinned and come short of the glory of God," Dr. Becker continues, "Baseball is a lot like that too. Baseball is a game of measuring things against impossible standards. There is no way to pretend success and there is no way to hide failure. It's all in the stats of, *The Book*."

She brings it down to the playing field. "An interesting thing about the stats is no one does very well. The very best hitters get about three hits in every ten tries. That's not a very good percentage for most jobs, but if you get three out of ten in baseball, they give you a million dollar salary. And if you do it several years in a row, they put you in the Hall of Fame.

Nobody is very good when measured against that absolute batting standard of 1,000. Everyone falls far short of it. No one has even come halfway to perfection in the course of a season. Paul, the apostle, would appreciate the similarities in the batting average standard and the inability of anyone to come anywhere near in living up to God's standard."

Dr. Becker, then tells of the grace that covers those errors. "In baseball, no matter how far behind your team may be, grace may come to bat for you. In the positive words of Yogi Berra, 'It ain't over 'til it's over.' In baseball there is always the possibility that something will happen. There is always a time for redemption."

To illustrate her words about grace, she gives an unusual example. "Take the case of Bob Brenly in 1986, playing third base for the San Francisco Giants. In the fourth inning of a game against the Atlanta Braves, Brenly made an error on a routine ground ball. Four batters later, he kicked away another grounder and then, while he was scrambling after the ball, he threw wildly past home plate trying to get the runner: three errors on the same play. A few minutes later he muffed yet another play to become the first player in the twentieth century to make four errors in one inning! Can you imagine what he felt like when he made that long walk to the dugout before all that crowd and teammates when the inning was finally over?

Then, in the bottom of the fifth, Brenly hit a home run. In the seventh, he hit a bases loaded single, to drive in two runs tying the game. And then, in the bottom of the ninth, Brenly came up to bat again with two outs. He ran the count to 3 and 2, and then hit a massive home run into the left field seats to win the game for the Giants!"

Dr. Becker concludes, "Jesus walked among us and spent much of his time with people who had gone 0 for 4 in life, as to speak in baseball terms; those who had dropped the ball, losers you might call them."

As a former Dodger, I must say, "We can't always come back a winner in our own strength and this is exactly what the grace of the Lord Jesus is all about." As Paul wrote, "Where sin multiplied, grace multiplied even more." The Bible also proclaims, "Love covers a multitude of sins."

Jesus came to seek and to save the lost! The grace of God brings forgiveness. Put your trust in Jesus for baseball is designed to break your heart and players know it's true.

Errors are part of the game. It doesn't take long for a player to realize he is prone to make mistakes and that he too, will make an error now and then.

Charles M. Schultz understands the inside of baseball brilliantly. His baseball cartoons are terrific! In his cartoon Peanuts, Charlie Brown and Lucy are playing baseball while Charlie Brown is pitching, the batter hits a Pop fly to Lucy and she immediately misses catching the ball. In discust Charlie Brown gives a "AAuch..Sound!"

He continues to scold Lucy "How could you miss such an easy fly ball?"

Lucy retorts, "The sun got into my eyes."

Out of frustration Charley Brown yells, "the sun isn't even out today, its cloudy!"

Lucy concludes in a sweet way, "The clouds got in my eyes."

I made an error, big time, in 1976, when I was pastor of the Far Hills Baptist Church, in Dayton, Ohio. One Sunday, after I delivered one of my baseball illustrated sermons, a few members urged me to demonstrate my pitching ability. I hesitated, but when they produced a ball and glove from a teenager, I impulsively said, "O.K., let's do it, now!"

The teenager was quickly signed-up to be my catcher. About a hundred curious members formed a gallery in two lines, like a bowling alley, on the church lawn. Even though at forty-one, nineteen years removed from my pro days, I felt confident that I could fire at least one pitch.

I removed my suit coat, loosened my tie, unbuttoned the top button of my white shirt and I was ready. Without a warm up, I took my stance like I was on the mound and let the ball fly – and did it fly! It soared, but, not to the catcher. That wild pitch went right into the crowd and hit one of our faithful men on the wrist. Wow, what a demonstration – a big time error! That was it for me; I never attempted to show my baseball prowess again.

Gary Graf tells us that even the great ones make glaring errors. In his book, *And God Said, "Play ball,"* he relates, "The great Babe Ruth himself ended the 1926 World Series by being thrown out trying to steal second base in the bottom of the ninth inning of the seventh and deciding game against the Cardinals. It should be noted that he represented the tying run."

Peter promised Jesus, he would die, rather than to deny him. At the trial, when Jesus needed him the most, he stood far away and denied his Lord. In fact, he denied him three times. He made the greatest error of his life!

After Jesus was condemned, crucified, buried and rose to life again, the messenger at the tomb said, "Go tell the disciples and Peter. . ." These words indicated Peter was now forgiven. This enabled Peter to stand on the Day of Pentecost and proclaim to thousands, "Jesus is alive! Everyone who calls on the name of the Lord will be saved." The grace of God allowed Peter to recover from his grave error.

> Grace, Grace, God's Grace
> Grace that will pardon and cleanse within.
> Grace, Grace, God's Grace
> Grace that is greater than all our sin.
> **Julia H. Johnston**

CHAPTER 12

IN PERFECT HARMONY

Tinker to Evers to Chance

Tinker to Evers to Chance
These are the saddest of possible words
Tinker to Evers to Chance
Trio of bear cubs and fleeter than birds
Tinker to Evers to Chance
Ruthlessly, pricking our gonfalon bubble,
Words that are weightier with nothing but trouble
Tinker to Evers to Chance
Franklin P. Adams

THE POEM, TINKER to Evers to Chance, immediately reminds many baseball fans of one of the most celebrated double-play combinations, ever played on the diamond. Joe Tinker was the shortstop, Johnny Evers played second base and Frank Chance held down the first base slot. This trio played in the Chicago infield from 1903 to 1913. They led the Chicago Cubs to three National League pennants and two World Series in the years, 1906 and 1908. All three players were enshrined in the Baseball Hall of Fame, not particularly because they were the best double play combo, but because they were lionized by Adams' poem.

The double play is the fastest play in baseball. From the time the ball is hit, two outs can be completed in less than five seconds. The keystone combination of the second baseman and the short stop working together, is the pathway to success.

These two players need to know each other's movements so well; they can throw the ball instantly and be assured that the other player will be at the bag ready to relay it on to first base. Because of the demand to work so closely together, many double play artists soon become friends off the diamond. In early baseball days these men roomed together, when the team was on the road.

Sadly, shortstop, Joe Tinker and second baseman, Johnny Evers, did not get along. According to Christine Ammer in her book, *Southpaws & Sunday Punches,* "They originally were good friends, but one day in 1908 Tinker got upset when Evers took a taxi to the ballpark and did not offer his friend a ride. The two quarreled and the argument ballooned out of proportion. For the next five years, until Tinker was traded to a different team, they continued their excellent fielding, but spoke only on the diamond and then only when absolutely necessary. The silence finally was broken in 1939 when they ran into each other at a Chicago radio station and made up their quarrel."

In the Bible, there were three teammates who started out together in a missionary journey. This trio seemed to be the perfect combination: Apostle Paul to John Mark to Barnabas. Paul was the experienced leader, John Mark the youthful energizer, and Barnabas the encourager. As they traveled, they came to Perga in Pamphylia. Abruptly, John Mark left them and went to Jerusalem. Even with John Mark's absence, Paul and Barnabas forged ahead.

When their difficult, but successful mission journey was completed, Paul and Barnabas returned to their home church at Antioch. Sometime later, Paul said to Barnabas, "Let's go back and visit the brothers in all the towns, where we preached the word of the Lord and see how they are doing." Barnabas wanted to take John Mark with them, but Paul did not think it wise, because he had deserted them on the first journey.

They had such a sharp disagreement, Paul and Barnabus divided company. So what could have been a success story of teammates, ended in disappointment. Barnabas with John Mark sailed for Cyprus, while Paul chose Silas to go with him to strengthen the new churches.

A few years later, like baseballers, Tinker and Evers, Paul and John Mark made up their differences. Paul asked, "Get John Mark and bring him with you, because he is helpful to me in my ministry."

Rick Warren in his insightful book, *The Purpose Driven Life,* underscores the actions of the ball players and missionaries alike, by saying, "Relationships are always worth restoring. The fellowship of the Church is more important than any individual's selfishness."

As a sophomore pitcher at Oklahoma University, Coach Jack Baer placed me in the starting pitching rotation ahead of junior pitcher George Loving. Suddenly, I felt a barrier between us. Our relationship was strained and we didn't find it comfortable speaking to each other. But then, there was a wonderful turnaround. I won my first college game against Iowa State, 5 to 4. The game came to a dramatic end, when my twin brother made a major league catch as the ball was going out of the park. Fred grabbed the top of the canvas covered wire fence with his left hand and scrambled up the side of it. Then, reaching with his gloved hand, he speared the ball as it was going over the fence. It was the game saver! To my complete surprise, George was the first one out of the dugout to congratulate me. It was a serendipitous moment! The barrier came down. Jesus said, "Blessed are the peace makers for they shall be called the children of God"

In Perfect Harmony

The catcher thinks first base play is a cinch,
And first baseman yearns to wear the mask-
Each player thinks he'd shine in other roles,
And grows disgusted with his daily task.
William A. Phelon

You need teammates working together to have a winning season. During a pioneer league game at Great Falls, Montana, I was on the mound against the Salt Lake City, Utah club. With runners at first and third, I threw a wild pitch that sent my catcher, Paul Stamen, chasing the ball toward the grand stands. The runner at third came charging home like a bull. Without hesitating, I ran toward home plate, just in time to catch the perfect throw from Stamen. With one swipe of the glove, I tagged the sliding runner out. Looking up, I spied the other runner, who was fifteen feet off first base. I was dumbfounded to find him stranded between first and second, but in an instant I threw the ball toward the first base bag thinking that our big first baseman, Andy Vanderveld, would be there, but he had charged in toward home. This could have turned into a baseball error disaster! But just like we had practiced time after time in spring training, Al Norris our second sacker, had automatically covered the empty first base. The runner was easily tagged out when he tried to get back to the base. It took four of us working together to make these two difficult plays look easy.

When you are playing, it's not all about you. Always keep in mind the other eight guys on the field. You can put it down, if you don't play together, you won't win. Baseball is a team sport. That means you stick together and rely on each other. Even players in the dugout are a real part of the team. This makes for relationships and loyalty.

The Bible is strong about working together. After Jesus called his disciples, he taught them to work as brothers, for he knew they needed each other. He never sent them out alone. His plan was, "two by two."

The early church listened to Christ's admonition, "They all joined together constantly in prayer, along with the women and Mary, the mother of Jesus and with his brothers." Some fifty days later, "When the day of Pentecost came, they were all together in one place." After Peter preached, 3,000 were baptized and added to the church. The apostle Paul admonished, "In Christ, we who are many, form one body and each member belongs to all the others."

Hugh Poland in his book, *Steal Away,* reminds us, "That the World Champion 1979 Pittsburg Pirates were referred to by the name of the popular song, 'We are Family.' This team of young players and veteran cast offs came together at the right time to win the Championship. Whenever that song is heard around the Pittsburg area, it reminds them of their beloved 1979 Pirates."

On several occasions, when I was pitching, I'd hear the opposing bench jockeys holler out, "You'd better pray, preacher!" One night I sure needed a prayer or two. I was on the mound, when my baseball blood got the best of me.

It happened in Pocatello, Idaho, when I was pitching against the Chicago Cubs farm team. We were leading, 3 to 1, in the seventh inning with two outs, when I walked a batter and the next guy hit a single. Manager, Lou Rochelle, pulled me to sit out the rest of the game on the bench. For some reason a Cubs player, who was coaching first base, began to make a few choice remarks to me about being knocked out of the game. One word led to another and before I realized it, I jumped out of the dugout and faced my opponent. He was as surprised as I and the next thing, we were going at it with fists flying.

It looked like a ferocious fight, but it was more the swing-and-miss variety, which soon became a poor wrestling match. I do remember, he bit me on the arm and, I guess, I had it coming, for I was pulling his hair.

As umpires, managers, and teammates came diving into the foray, it got out of hand. Dozens of fans jumped out of the stands and spilled onto the field. Within in a few moments the security guards restored peace. But just as we were being ejected from the game, the Cubs player gave me a parting fist to my right eye.

As I sat dejectedly in the club house all alone, I felt ashamed of myself. Here I was a "baseball preacher" and look what I had done! After the game, my teammates came trooping in. I did my best to give an apologetic speech, but my faithful combatants cheerfully drowned out my efforts with their rendition of, "For He's a Jolly Good Fellow!" Our big first baseman, Andy Vanderveld said, "I knew it had to be a good fight because our preacher was in it." For the first time, I felt truly accepted as a "preacher teammate."

The next day, I was interviewed on television, sporting a prominent black eye and scrapes on my face. Of course they were focused on the fight and my reactions as a one-day-to-be-preacher. "Well," I said, "The only thing I ever got out of a fight is this black eye. But since you mentioned me as a future preacher, let me tell you," if I can't preach Christ to 'em,' I'll beat the devil out of 'em."

Major League baseball, from its beginning, was for white teammates only. Segregation was the norm of the day and "equal, but separate" ruled the diamonds. The Negro League had players of tremendous abilities and drew great crowds, but were denied the chance to be teammates in the Majors. Baseball was so popular, it was the perfect medium for talented ballplayers to be instrumental in the needed social change.

John Thorn was right on target in his colossal book, *Total Baseball,* when he wrote, "Major League baseball became a major front in the ongoing battle for racial equality. That year, 1947, Branch Rickey's 'great experiment' introduced Jackie Robinson as the first known black player in the Majors." History will always place them together.

Carl Erskine, teammate of Jackie, writes in his book, *Tales from the Dodger Dugout,* "Branch Rickey was a genius in reading not only talent of a baseball prospect, but also his attitude and aptitude. Jackie's impact on America in its struggle to allow every citizen the same civil rights, proved he belonged and he helped to open hearts and minds."

Jackie's entrance with the Brooklyn Dodgers, paved the way for more than one-hundred African-Americans and black Hispanics to play in the major leagues in the next decade. According to Carolyn Butler, writing for *Smithsonian magazine,* "Over the next twelve seasons, African-Americans including, Robinson, Roy Campanella, Willie Mays and Hank Aaron, won Rookie of the Year and nine Most Valuable Player awards. In the same article, Raymond Doswell, curator of the Negro Leagues Baseball Museum in Kansas City, Missouri said, "These guys had been playing ball all their lives - they were older than typical rookies, they knew the game and what they had to adjust to was off the field, for the most part," On August 21, 2010, The United States Postal Service commemorated the Negro Leagues (1920 – 1960) with a folio of illustrated action baseball stamps.

But, Jackie stood alone in his rookie year under tremendous pressure from opposing teams, spectators, the media, top baseball brass and even players from his team. *Fascinating baseball Facts, by David Nemec and Pete Palmer,* gives the picture of the terrible animosity he faced. "Sportswriter Jimmy Powers penned about Jackie Robinson as a rookie, 'Robinson will not make the grade in the major leagues. He is a thousand-to-one shot at best. The Negro players simply don't have the brains or the skills'." Jimmy Powers was one thousand percent wrong! Jackie was such a sensation in his first year, he was voted, "Rookie of the Year" hands down. Yet, if any player needed a sympathetic teammate, it was Jackie.

On the first road trip to Cincinnati in 1947, spectators began chanting racial epithets from the stands. George Vecsey wrote in his in-depth book, *Baseball,* "Reece put his arm around Robinson's shoulder, to demonstrate, in Reece's part of the world, that they were teammates and equals." This was a significant gesture for second baseman, Pee Wee Reese, because he was a true southern gentleman from Louisville,

Kentucky. Throughout the season, when the Dodgers would go on the road, Jackie became the object of fierce taunting and catcalls. Time and again, second baseman, Pee Wee would calmly walk over to Jackie at first base and put his arm around his shoulder." Jackie never forgot it!

A statue was unveiled, November 1, 2005, in Brooklyn's Coney Island Key Span Park, depicting Reece putting his arm around Robinson's shoulder. Teammates, black and white Dodgers, together!

From Teammates

Outlined on a sea of green grass
Stood these two great athletes
One black, One white,
both wearing the same
Team uniform.
Peter Golenbock

When Jesus was giving the truth of the joy and essence of life, he makes reference to the greatest love of all. "Greater love has no one than this that he lay down his life for his friends."

Another ball player on that Dodger team who befriended Jackie was outstanding pitcher, Carl Erskine, in a recent news article, Erskine, now 92, pointed to his Christian faith as his foundation in welcoming Robinson. "Jackie was made in the image of God, so I treated him with dignity and respect."

It was July 15 1947, when over 26,000 fans, half the crowd were black fans who came to see Jackie play his first game in Major League Baseball. The last few years on July 15 Jackie's number 42 is worn on the shirts of every player in the Majors.

Our Dodger farm club in Reno, Nevada, had several teammates who were black. Nate Smith, from Detroit, was the best battery mate who caught for me. He was an articulate, intelligent college man and a serious ball player. His quiet, friendly ways were well received by the team. Only one time, Nate came to the mound to question me about my refusal to accept his pitch call. I should have listened to him! My pitch caused a missile shot over the head of our shortstop, Charley Smith. Nate eventually was sold to the Baltimore Orioles and in 1962, spent that season catching for the big club. He has always been a credit to baseball.

Another black player I enjoyed, was outfielder Tommy "hot foot" Humber, the California State league's top stolen base stealer. In personality, he was just the opposite of Nate. He was a happy-go-lucky, devil-may-care kind of guy. He lived a different life style from Nate and me, but was a good teammate. We all enjoyed his remarks in the dugout and club house. To the surprise of Joyce and me, he once introduced his girlfriend as, "My main squeeze."

For us race was not treated as politically sensitive. When we put on those Dodger uniforms, we were all one race - baseball players. We had banded together as brothers. One for all and all for one! When we lost, we all lost; when we won, we all won.

Jerry Craft and Kathleen Sullivan have put together a true account in their book, *Our White Boy,* of racial harmony in a time of racial distrust. Craft, tells the story of how he became the first white man to play in the West Texas Colored League, during the summers of 1959 and 1960. It was a Jackie Robinson account in reverse.

Carl Sedberry, manager of the Wichita/Graham Stars, had a good team of offense and defense, but no pitching. In the midst of the civil rights movement, Sedberry telephoned Craft, a white Texas Tech student and excellent pitcher. He invited him to try out for the team and offered Craft seventy-five dollars a game.

When the pitcher showed up for the game and saw only black people in the parking lot, in the stands and a black team taking warm-ups, he thought he had the wrong stadium and date. He was about to leave, when Mr. Sedberry walked toward him and introduced himself as the manager and the caller.

Craft was more than a little surprised but reluctantly, decided to at least give it a try.

"His new teammates were equally slow to embrace Craft," writes Brice Cherry of *The Waco Tribune-Herald*. "They didn't call him by name, but rather, 'White Boy' and it wasn't a compliment."

Cherry continues, "On the way home after a game in Waco, the team stopped at a small black restaurant. All the patrons were looking at Craft and the guy who owned the restaurant came over and said, 'Sir,

I don't want any trouble, but you're going to have to leave … because you're white. My customers don't want you here.'

The owner told Sedberry that he and the players could stay, but Craft would have to leave. But when Craft rose to head outside, the entire team followed. All of them left their suppers sitting there and we were hungry."

Craft said, "Bobby Harem was our right fielder … he smiled and threw his arm around me and said, 'Welcome to our world'." With every win, the name "White Boy" began to give way to "Our White Boy."

This was the beginning of two summers of uncharted waters for the only white player in an all black league. Mark W. Stamm, of Southern Methodist University wrote, "Jerry Craft and his black teammates traveled, talked, dined, and faced fear and humiliation together."

Jesus was never prejudiced. "Whoever" was always his call for discipleship. However, one of the early New Testament churches had a prejudice problem. Race was not a factor but the Jerusalem church showed hesitation in accepting believing non-Jews into their fellowship. Many Greeks and Romans, who were called Gentiles, had become Christians under the preaching ministry of Paul and Barnabas.

Since the Jerusalem church was comprised of only converted Jews, they had a philosophy, a non-Jew had to first go through a Jewish ceremonial ritual before they could be a Christian. It took a special meeting led by former Jews, the apostle Paul and Barnabas, to convince the Jerusalem congregation to open their minds and hearts. At the conference, the church accepted the believers without the Jewish ceremonial rite. The Jerusalem church was so pleased with their decision, they immediately sent a letter to their Gentile brothers, "The apostles and elders, your brothers, to the Gentile believers in Antioch, Syria and Cilicia, Greetings!"

Billy Sunday, famed evangelist, played in the outfield for the Chicago Cubs and the Pittsburg Pirates from 1883-1890. His testimony printed in *The Omaha Daily News,* in October, 1915, gives his heart-felt need for friends. "I walked down a street in Chicago with some of the team. Across the street a company of men and women (Salvation Army) were playing on instruments. A young man stepped out and said, 'We are going down to the Pacific Garden Mission. Won't you come with us?'

I got up and said to my teammates, 'I'm through; I'm going to Jesus Christ.' Some of them laughed and some mocked me: but one gave me encouragement: others never said a word.

The next day I had to get out to the ballpark and practice. I never slept that night. I was afraid of the horse laugh that gang would give me because I had taken my stand for Jesus Christ.

I walked down to the old ball grounds. I slipped my key into the wicker gate and the first man to meet me after I got inside was Mike Kelly. 'Bill, I'm proud of you! Religion is not my long suit, but I'll help you if I can.' Up came Cap Anson, the best ball player that ever played the game: Pfeffer, Clarsson, Flint, Jimmy McCormack, Burns, Williamson and Dalrymple. There wasn't a fellow in that gang who knocked: every teammate had a word of encouragement for me."

True Friends

True friends are like jewels,
Yet more precious,
For gold cannot drive them away.
Come sorrow and pain,
Come the wind and rain,
There by your side, they remain.
Hard luck drives away the pretenders,
The fair feathered friends disappear.
But true to the last, good friends stand fast,
There by your side, in friendship's name.
Unknown

Baseball teammate's friendship often goes far beyond the diamond and continues throughout life. Carl Erskine, gives a personal touch. "Gil Hodges and I were both from Indiana. We were both scouted by Stan Feezle of Indianapolis and played together for a decade in Brooklyn and Los Angeles. One of my fondest memories of Ebbets Field was hearing Gladys Gooding, our organist, play 'Back Home Again in Indiana.'

Following Gil's playing days; he became an outstanding manager and led the 1969 Mets to the Cinderella World Series championship.

Then the shock came in the spring of 1972, when he died suddenly, of a massive heart attack at age fifty-one.

Several of us attended his funeral as honorary pallbearers. At the conclusion of the service, we followed the closed casket as it was wheeled outside of the church. At that moment the organist played 'Back Home again in Indiana.' That really hit me hard. I was so choked up that I couldn't speak, not even to Howard Cosell, waiting with his camera crew."

The apostle Paul was once a terrible threat to the early church. In his own words, "for I am the least of the apostles and do not even deserve to be called an apostle, because I persecuted the church of God." In fact, he gave approval to the stoning death of the good and courageous man, Stephen.

Therefore, the church was extremely suspicious and afraid to welcome Paul into the fellowship, even though he testified that he had been converted on the road to Damascus. Before God dealt with him on that journey, he used the Hebrew name Saul; afterwards, he was called by his Gentile name Paul. However, to the Jerusalem church, the new Paul was the same old Saul.

If any man needed a "teammate," it was the outsider, Paul. So Barnabas, like Pee Wee Reese, put his arm around Paul and welcomed him to the fellowship. As Christian baseball historian, Hugh Poland, affirms in his book, *Steal Away,* "Paul went on the great missionary journeys and many of his letters to the congregations he founded became part of the Christian Scriptures. His ministry opened the door for men and women, of all races and nationalities, to hear and receive the love of Christ."

Teammates often give each other nicknames and some stick a lifetime. There is a lot of camaraderie among players, so nicknames are prevalent. When George Herman Ruth, pitched for the Boston Red Sox as a young rookie, they called him, "Babe," and throughout history, even beyond baseball, it has been his personal identification. There are more nicknames given to baseball players than any other sport and the reason may be because the season is longer and they play more games. A ball player is fortunate to have a nickname, because it's usually a term of endearment. Baseball is loaded with names that immediately bring to mind a certain player:

Nickname	Player	Nickname	Player
Babe	George Herman Ruth	Chipper	Larry Jones
Ryan Express	Nolan Ryan	Hammer Henry	Hank Aaron
Yogi	Lawrence Berra	Flying Dutchman	Honus Wagner
Catfish	Catfish Hunter	Georgia Peach	Ty Cobb
Big Mac	Mark McGwire	Dizzy	Dizzy Dean
Big Puma	Lance Berkman	The Iron Horse	Lou Gehrig
Big Unit	Randy Johnson	A-Rod	Alex Rodriquez
The Evangelist	Billy Sunday	Christian Gentleman	Mattewson
Mr. October	Reggie Jackson	Tom Terrific	Tom Seaver
Mr. November	Derek Jeter	Satchel	Leroy Paige
Stan the Man	Stanley Musial	Pee Wee	Harold Reese
Say Hey	Willie Mays	Joltin Joe	Joe DiMaggio
Mo	Mariano Rivera	Shoeless Joe	Joe Jackson

The Bible has a number of people who can be identified by their nicknames:

Nickname	Player	Nickname	Player
The twin	Thomas	The Beloved	John
The brother	James	The Traitor	Judas
The Rock	Peter	Sons of Thunder	James and John
Old Fox	King Herrod	the Baptist	John
The Nazarene	Jesus	The Son of Man	Jesus
The Son of God	Jesus	Rabbi	Jesus
Tax Collector	Matthew	The Zealot	Simon

Every current Major League team has a nickname. Sporting journalists, broadcasters, and fans usually refer to teams by them. Many of the names are so established, that newspapers routinely use them in headlines. The older established teams are the best known among fans and spectators. In order, here are the most popular:

1. New York Yankees
2. Los Angeles Dodgers
3. Chicago Cubs
4. St. Louis Cardinals
5. Boston Red Sox
6. Cincinnati Reds
7. Detroit Tigers
8. San Francisco Giants

The Tampa Bay team found the devil didn't help them. After ten seasons, Tampa Bay dropped "devil" from their nickname and brought in the ray of sunshine from the sea. Their logo is the flapping stingray and now they call themselves The Tampa Bay Rays. With that, they won a World Series!

Nicknames are not always endearing. Sometimes they describe a certain distinction about a player's personality, ability or appearance. When I was a rookie in spring training at Vero Beach, I was six foot and weighed 170 pounds. My nickname, "bird legs" almost stuck. I can still hear those "cat calls" from the bench, "Hey Minton, do your legs swell up like that every spring?" My twin's nickname was "Road Runner." He was a daring base stealer.

Nicknames which are somewhat negative have stuck and yet ball players have distinguished themselves, in spite of them. Some, even came to enjoy the slander. Kevin Summers is one of those. Now a successful businessman in Dallas, he was dubbed by his high school sports reporter, "E5" (error by third baseman). Summers told me "I had a terrible game at third. I kicked a ball away, because of a bad hop and then dropped a fly ball because of the glare of the sun in my eyes. That nickname, E5, stuck with me through high school and college playing days. Even today, I hear, 'Hey, E5, how's everything going?' I've come to enjoy it."

Nickname	Player	Nickname	Player
Three Fingers	Mordecai Brown	Lippy	Leo Durocher
Old Tomato Face	Gabby Hartnett	Ducky Wucky	Joe Medwick
Bonehead	Fred Merkle	Pee Wee	Harold Reece
Shoeless Joe	Joe Jackson	Penquin	Ron Cey

Surprisingly, the name Christian is not the name that Jesus used for his followers. He called them disciples, brothers, and friends. The name Christian was given as a nickname, in contempt, "first at Antioch." The secular writers of that day indicate that the citizens of Antioch used nicknames rather freely.

The word Christian literally means, "Christus," or Little Christ, which was the last thing that true believers want to portray. *The Fausset Brown Commentary,* states, "At first, believers had no distinctive name, but were called among themselves 'brethren,' 'disciples,' 'those in the way,' 'saints,' and by the Jews, with contempt, 'Nazarenes.' Since they could no longer be looked upon as a Jewish sect, the Gentiles designated the believers by the new name 'Christians'." It is to be noted, the name Christian appears in only three places in the Bible and each time is spoken with derision: Acts 11:26, Acts 26:28, and 1 Peter 4:16.

The nickname Christian, was no doubt an implication of scorn, as in King Agrippa's statement "Paul, do you think that in such a short time you can persuade me to be a Christian?" When Peter wrote, "However, if you suffer as a Christian, do not be ashamed, but praise God that you bear that name." Throughout the ages, this nickname of derision has been worn with dignity, honor, sacrifice, persecution and death!

In the early 1970's, when the "Jesus Movement" was sweeping across our nation, I was pastoring the growing Southcliff Baptist church in Fort Worth, Texas. One Sunday a fine couple visited our church from California. They had been saved in one of the "Jesus Movement" camp style meetings. Church was yet to be part of their religious life style.

Their non-conforming ways made some of our church members nervous. But our people soon found out they were true believers!

Tony Romeo was a good looking athletic man, former football player with the Boston Patriots. Sabra was a beautiful statuesque blond with a lovely singing voice. As the couple visited each Sunday it didn't take long before they became favorites among our people.

It was a joyous Christian day when I baptized them!

Pastoring a church was not the same as pitching but both held its own excitement! Happiness is winning a tough ball game! Joy is leading a person to a saving knowledge of Christ!

I was called as senior pastor of the great Tower Grove Baptist Church in St. Louis, Missouri. To my surprise and disappointment, this inner city church had no black members. I couldn't believe that my Dodger baseball team was twenty-five years ahead in carrying out the Bible admonition, "Whosoever will, may come!"

It wasn't long, before we started a bus ministry, picking up kids in the neighborhood and bringing them to Sunday school and our new Christian Life Center. This brought in black children as well. The bus ministry worked like a Dodgers, "clean sweep." Our congregation accepted into the fellowship, the black children and their parents.

Every Sunday morning, at the close of both worship services, the congregation held hands and sang this Christian ballad. This brings back blessed times and memories.

We are one in the Spirit
We are one in the Lord
We are one in the Spirit
We are one in the Lord

And they'll know we are Christians
by our love, by our love
Yes, they'll know we are Christians
by our love, by our love.

We will walk with each other
We will walk hand in hand,
We will walk with each other
We will walk hand in hand.
And together, we'll spread the news,
that God is in the land,
And they'll know we are Christians
by our love, by our love.
And they'll know we are Christians
by our love.
Peter Scholte

CHAPTER 13

IT AIN'T NOTHIN' TILL I SAY SO!

There once was an umpire whose vision
Was cause for abuse and derision.
He remarked in surprise,
Why pick on my eyes?
It's my heart that dictates my decision.
Ogden Nash

"I JUST COST THAT kid a perfect game!" umpire Jim Joyce told news reporters, immediately after seeing his miscall on replay. His call cost Detroit pitcher, Armando Galarraga, a perfect game against the Cleveland Indians, June 2, 2010. Galarraga, in the top of the ninth, was one out away from a perfect game, 27 up and 27 down, when the American League umpire blew one of the biggest calls of baseball. "I thought he beat the throw. I was convinced he beat the throw, until I saw the replay." It was a bad call by a good umpire.

The next day Detroit's manager Jim Leyland arranged for pitcher Galarraga to take the Tigers line up card to umpire Joyce at home plate to start the pregame proceedings. The umpire fought back tears and patted the pitcher's shoulder as he accepted the card from the conciliatory pitcher, who smiled and said, "I know nobody's perfect."

Umpires are the most unloved people on the baseball field; yet without these dark-blue clothed figures, the games could not continue. Baseball regards umpires as a necessary evil. Harry Wendelstedt, a veteran Major league umpire agrees, "If they could play games without us, the majority would vote to do so." Even though he possesses the final authority on the playing field; as an old adage states, "No one ever paid his way into a ball game to watch the umpires."

The long time trilogy of umpiring is caught in these phrases: "I calls 'em likes I sees 'em, I calls 'em like they are," and as Bill Guthrie, early time umpire, summed it up, "It ain't nothin' till I say so."

Major League umpire, Durwood Merrill, gives an honest word about the men in blue from his book, *You're Out and you're Ugly Too!* "I'll tell you this about umpires. When the time comes to play ball, you won't find a more honest foursome anywhere. You can't say that about politicians, doctors, lawyers, and certainly not golfers. That kind of honesty doesn't exist anywhere else."

> From the benches, black with people, there went up a muffled roar,
> Like the beating of the storm-waves on a stern and distant shore,
> "Kill him! Kill the umpire!" shouted someone on the stands;
> And it's likely they'd a-killed him had not Casey raised his hand.
> **Ernest Lawrence Thayer**

Fans were over the edge rowdy in baseball's early stages and surprisingly it was accepted by the general public as freedom of expression. The 1890 baseball rule book gave umpires some respect by stating, he must be called, "Mr. Umpire." But the Anti-umpire sentiment continued on into the 1890's with one of the most popular players of the day, Al Spaulding, summing it up: "Fans who despise umpires are simply showing their democratic right to protest against tyranny."

This popular 1886 poem, gives the evidence.

> Mother, may I slug the umpire,
> May I slug him right away,
> So he cannot be here, Mother,
> When the clubs begin to play?
> Let me mop the ground up, Mother
> With his person, dearest, do;
> If the ground can stand it, Mother
> I don't see why you can't, too
> **Chicago Tribune**

Bruce Weber, in his exhaustive umpire book, *As They See 'Em*, writes how this umpire baiting brought a real concern from across the Atlantic. "In 1928, an Italian newspaper, *L'osservatore Romano*, used the venomous cries of American baseball fans to argue, that Christian values in the New World had devolved into paganism, a literal interpretation of 'Kill the Umpire." That might have been laughable if the New York Times, in an editorial, hadn't found it necessary to explain the national custom. Their rebuttal trying to distinguish between literal and figurative expressions of rage ran a headline that read, 'We don't really mean it'."

I was a character in my high school's presentation of Mark Twain's great novel, "A Connecticut Yankee in King Arthur's Court," in which the umpire was part of the play. Twain was trying to get his knights of the round table to become knowledgeable about baseball but he had trouble when picking low ranked men to be umpires. The umpire's were so badly treated, that none of them survived a game. Thus, he had to pick those of higher rank and lofty positions to insure government protection.

Bruce Weber gives the most dramatic example of violence against an umpire, when Billy Evans, Hall of Famer, in 1907, received a concussion when he was struck by a thrown bottle full of beer. This attitude against umpires generally persisted well into the middle of the twentieth century. Even in 1955 it was acceptable to heap scorn on the poor umpire according to the Broadway musical, *Damn Yankees*.

> The Umpire, the umpire,
> the guy who calls every play,
> We ain"t got no use for the umpire
> unless he calls 'em our way.
> **Richard Adler and Jerry Ross**

Jesus Christ was often placed in an "umpire" position when Pharisees and others tried to trick him. "We know you are a man of integrity and you teach the way of God in accordance with the truth. You aren't swayed by men, because you pay no attention to who they are. Tell us then, what is your opinion? Is it right to pay taxes to Caesar or not?" But Jesus, knowing of their evil intent said, "Why are you trying to trap me? Show me the coin used for paying the tax." They brought him a denarius, and he asked them, "Whose portrait is this and whose inscription?"

"Caesar's," they replied. Then he said to them, "Give to Caesar what is Caesar's, and to God what is God's."

It is interesting, at the beginning of baseball; umpires worked for free and were well respected. In fact, in the earliest days, being chosen as an umpire was an honor and there was never a thought of paying him for his services. The word, "umpire," comes from the French nounpere, meaning, "a non- peer," not an equal, one who decides disputes between equals. It can be said of nearly all umpires, "Umpires don't root; they only look." The role of the umpire is to ensure that decisions are fair.

In 1876, the National League gave the edict, "The umpire is the sole judge of play, and is entitled to the respect of the spectators, and any person hissing or hooting at, or offering any insult or indignity of him, must be promptly ejected from the grounds." It was a worthy try, but it had no way of enforcement, so it was of non-affect. Today, the home team management is in charge of unruly spectators.

Derek Gentile, writes in his book, *Spitters, squeezes, and steals,* "Nineteenth century umpires had no dress code but dressed as if they might be going to church. They wore top hats, stylish topcoats, spats, and carried a cane. The effect was to deliver a message that they were gentlemen who expected ballplayers and fans to act in a civil way." By 1910 umpires began to wear the dark blue uniforms that are worn today.

When baseball went professional in the 1870's, the game became more competitive, increasing the need for stronger neutral observers to keep the peace on the field. It then became the most thankless and too often dangerous job in baseball, because of rowdy players, pushy coaches and unforgiving fans. When an umpire makes an unpopular decision, he is perhaps the most disliked man on the planet. Internet's Baseball Almanac gives Milton Bracker's Poem, printed in the New York Times, a real look at the ump's plight.

The Umpire

The umpire is a lonely man
Whose calls are known to every fan
Yet none will call him Dick or Dan
In all the season's games.
Milton Bracker

Mike Shannon, *Tales from the Dugout,* gives a heart rendering event that shows fans warm respect and concern for those men in blue. "On opening day in Cincinnati, Ohio in 1996, during a game against The Montreal Expos home-plate umpire John McSherry died of sudden cardiac arrest, only seven pitches into the game at Riverfront Stadium. McSherry collapsed and fell prostrate, face down, still wearing his mask and chest protector. The Reds trainers, team physicians, Montreal trainers and at least three other doctors attending the game, who vaulted from the stands arrived within seconds to minister to the fallen umpire. As stunned silence reigned throughout the ballpark, they worked frantically on McSherry for a quarter of an hour, but all attempts to revive him were unsuccessful.

The players on both teams were too upset to concentrate on baseball and felt, moreover, that the proper thing to do would be to postpone the game, out of respect for the universally liked McSherry. Reds shortstop, Barry Larkin put the player's feelings into words, 'In good conscience, out of respect for life, I can't go out there'."

Writer Shannon continued, "The following day saw a rare, if not another unique, event in baseball history. As the umpires walked onto the field prior to the start of the makeup game, Cincinnati fans showered them with a standing ovation that expressed sympathy, understanding, and appreciation. Flags at major league ballparks flew half-mast for the rest of the week and the National League umpires wore black armbands on their uniform shirts all season."

Regardless of feelings that run high, the integrity of the game should be everyone's concern, which is why umpires are paid to safeguard it. Too often, in the minds of baseball enthusiast's, winning trumps fair play. Umpires are often quoted, "If they played by the honor system, they wouldn't need us."

More than fair play was necessary in the epic Bible account that revealed the good judgment of King Solomon. Two prostitutes had each given birth to sons a few days apart. One of the babies died suddenly in the night, so the mother of the dead child exchanged her baby for the living one. The next morning, the unsuspecting mother realized that there had been an exchange and tried to get her baby back, but to no avail. The case was brought to the king. Upon hearing the dilemma, the king said, "Bring me a sword."

He gave the order, "Cut the living child in two and give half to each." The true mother cried out, "Give her the baby! Don't kill him!" The king then handed the baby boy to his real mother. King Solomon's verdict was right and fair and all Israel marveled at his judgment

In early baseball games, only one person umpired the game. The umpire usually stood or knelt in foul territory along the first base line. In 1903, The Book gave permission for the umpire "to stand anywhere on the field he likes." As the games progressed, players began to take advantage of the poor umpire. Often times, a runner on first base, seeing that the ump's back was turned to watch the play in progress, would cut across the diamond, not touching second and land upon third. *Baseball Anecdotes* by David Okrent and Steve Wulf, reported, "A player was called out while standing on third base. The surprised base runner asked, 'Why?' The ump retorted, "Because, you got there too soon."

In 1876, an official baseball ruling was made, "If an umpire is unable to see whether a catch has been fairly made, he may ask the spectators and players about it and then make his decision." That rule was reversed six years later in 1882. Finally, in 1933, it was ruled that three umpires were to be assigned to every major league regular game. Now, a typical Major League game is overseen by an umpire-in-chief and three field umpires.

Parents don't realize what they are teaching their children by their nonsense in the stands: screaming at the umpires, gestures of disappointment when their child or other players don't do well on the field of play and being hostile toward other team's players.

The Bible says, "Train a child in the way he should go and when he is old he will not depart from it." Actually, the most difficult word for a parent to say is "no" because you have to explain it. "Yes" is easy for usually there is no explanation necessary.

Only the umpires don't have to explain their calls! Out, safe, strike, ball with the exception of technology.

In the Bible, Moses was the lone judge of the land. His father-in-law, Jethro, asked, "Why, are you alone sitting as judge, while all the people stand around you from morning until evening?"

Moses replied, "Because the people come to me to inquire of God. Whenever they have a dispute, they come to me for a decision between them." Jethro said, "This is not good, you and your people will wear out, for the task is too heavy. You can't do it alone. You remain God's appointed leader, but you should select able, God-fearing men who are trustworthy, and hate bribes who will be judges of the minor cases. Every important case will be brought to you." Moses listened to his father-in-law and did everything he said.

There are more than one hundred thousand volunteer and/or paid baseball umpires. These umpires are mailmen, school teachers, shop clerks, executives, gardeners, sales people, life guards, and a few preachers. They call balls and strikes for little league, high school and college games. Most of them do it for the love of the game and those who play it. Basically, they would starve to death, if they depended on umpire's pay.

Joe Kearney, is one of those thousands of umpires who work amateur baseball games. In a conversation at Sugar Creek Baptist church, I found that this guy not only loves baseball, but he loves umpiring with a passion! At his own expense, he has gone to an umpiring school in Florida, where hopeful professionals are trained. At fifty-two, he has no aspirations of being a professional. "I just like to help this great sport to be played fair and square for the enjoyment of the players and fans alike." His three years of umpiring give him a good insight into the complexity of the task, "The most difficult things are to keep an accurate pitch count and keeping your head in the game as it progresses. The game itself causes us to make decisions at times that seem impossible to call." He concluded our conversation with these inspiring words, "For me, it's more than a hobby, it's a calling."

A special medal of bravery needs to be placed upon the chests of umps, like Joe, who call those little league and even high school games.

Sometimes their lives seem to be in danger, not from the ire of the players or coaches, but from dear mom and dad in the stands.

The Huffington Iowa Post printed this sports banner June 13, 2009, "Don Briggs, umpire, ejects crowd during baseball game." The article went on to report, "An umpire has emptied the stands of more than a hundred fans for being unruly at the high school baseball game between Winfield-Mount Union and West Burlington. After a forty minute delay, fans returned and the game resumed. West Burlington won the game twelve to eleven.

Perry Barbara, fifty-six, is a hit as an umpire, even though she never played the game. After reading books about baseball she decided to launch out into umpiring at age twenty-nine and landed a job with Little League games. She told *AARP Magazine* writer, Pat Jordan, "I get an adrenaline rush when I walk out to home plate." Barbara's career has expanded to about everything from high school games to Major League exhibitions. In one of her first games, Barbara, was practically booed off the field for calling a foul ball fair. But she is not alone, for umpires all agree that one of the hardest plays to call is one down the line near the outfield fence. In fact, in 2008, a rash of miscalled home run balls led baseball, for the first time, to use replay to help big league umps make their decision.

A few days ago, I watched on TV a game between the Yankees and the Angels in Anaheim, California. Even though it was a bright sunny day, it took five minutes for the four umpires, with the use of replay, to declare that Torii Hunter's hit was a home run instead of a foul ball.

Bruce Weber gives the account of his dilemma of getting the call right on a long hit near the left field line. "It was a still night with a dim haze hovering above the field and I was behind the plate. When the batter swung and lined the ball toward the left-field corner, I leaped out from behind the catcher and straddled the third-base line and immediately knew I was in trouble ... About halfway out to the fence, the ball disappeared in the haze and I lost it completely. I didn't see it land: I didn't see it roll. The last I knew the ball was in the air, well in fair territory, but like a lot of hard-hit balls pulled by right-handed hitters, hooking with a sharp grace toward the line."

Weber went on to write, "I guessed. With a fifty percent chance, I called it fair and got it woefully, haplessly, disastrously wrong. I knew right away, from the hysterical disbelief of the team in the field, that I'd blown it. (A hint for umpires: In such a case, when you really don't know, call it foul. That way, if you're wrong, you've caused less damage.)"

Jesus was often asked questions that were, "foul balls." On one occasion, as he walked with his disciples they saw a man blind from birth. They asked, "Rabbi, who sinned, this man or his parents, that this man is born blind?"

Jesus answered, "Neither this man nor his parents but this happened so that the work of God might be displayed in his life." Having said this, he spit on the ground, made some mud with the saliva, and put it on the man's eyes. "Go wash in the Pool of Siloam." So the man went and washed, and came home seeing.

When I played, it was difficult to have friendship with the umpires. Somehow, I felt they were more enemy than any thing else. They were offish, on and off the field and I never remembered seeing them in the hotels or restaurants we frequented. They were like desert nomads living somewhere beyond us. In our minor league games they worked in pairs, so they spent their days together, away from the baseball clubs. When they came to the ball park in their game blue uniforms, they seemed much older than us. Yet, when I did have the chance to talk with them, I found them to be only a little older and furthermore, they seemed refreshingly honest; just regular guys!

Harry "Steamboat" Johnson, minor league umpire for thirty-six years is quoted, "An umpire leads a lonely life. He has few human contacts, save with his partner. He is as isolated as a monk in a monastery."

After the game, I'd go over the plays in my mind as to how I could have pitched better. The umps confessed they did the same thing about their calls. It bothered me to have a poorly pitched game and they were also bothered about a questionable game call.

Durwood Merrill who was an American League umpire for thirty years wrote, "I've kicked my share of calls. Fortunately, they didn't occur during a big postseason game, or on national television. But I made mistakes, just like the rest of my peers.

I was having a bad game night when Detroit manager, Sparky Anderson, came running out of the dugout. Sparky has a pretty even temperament. But on this night, he was mad. He started chewing on me and I said, 'I know, I know.' He said, 'What do you mean, you know?' I said, 'Look, Sparky, I'm not going to get no better.' Sparky shook his head, smiled, and said, 'Well, I guess I'm not going to get no better, either.' With that, he turned and ran back to the dugout.

Like ball players, minor league umpires are trying to move up to the big time, level by level. In the minors, there are approximately two hundred umpires who aspire to earn one of the sixty or more Major League positions. Their goals and hopes are not helped much by their pay, which, is just above the salary of better paid minor league players. Umpires work ten to twelve years in the minors before being ready for the majors.

Regardless of where they officiate, umpires represent baseball and have the responsibility for upholding the dignity of the game. They are not always right but as one umpire put it, "I never missed one in my heart," To me, that meant he had good judgment and could be trusted.

Jesus was understood that way. Whether the people that milled around him liked him or not, they knew he had sound, honest judgment. The scribes and the Pharisees brought a woman caught in adultery, making her stand in front of him. "Teacher," they said, "In the law, Moses commanded us to stone such women. So, what do you say?" They asked this question to trap him, to have evidence to accuse him.

Jesus stooped down and started writing on the ground with his finger. He stood up and said to them, "The one without sin among you should be the first to throw a stone at her." When they heard this they walked away. Jesus was left with the woman and said to her, "Woman, where are they? Has no one condemned you?" "No one, Lord," she answered. "Neither do I condemn you," said Jesus, "Go, and sin no more." Even though the decision was dramatic, Jesus never heaped attention on himself.

Most umpires strive to be unnoticed and anonymous. In reality, umpires are baseball's invisible people. Bud Selig, former Commissioner of Major League Baseball said, "One of the best days an umpire can have is if nobody knows he's there." It's routine but meaningful; umpires are the first to vacate the field after the game is over. Before the baseball crowd can realize it, the umps are gone as if they had vanished into thin air!

The Bible gives clear evidence that Jesus, over and over tried to keep out of the limelight. After Jesus had fed the five thousand, the crowd wanted to announce to the world that he was their popular choice. "When Jesus knew they were about to come and take him by force to make him king, he withdrew again to the mountain by himself."

Throughout baseball history, umpires have stood their ground, mostly in silence, and have proven themselves worthy of their vested authority. Every major league game is televised, as well as many games in the minor leagues. Surprisingly, television replays, even in slow motion, have become a friend of the men in blue. In most cases, even in those bang, bang plays, that demand a split-second decision, the accuracy of the umps' calls have been verified. All must agree, umps are not as blind as biased fans. To quote the Pogo comic strip phrase: "We have found the enemy and he is us!" It is amazing how emotion can trick our eyes.

After Babe Ruth was called out on strikes, he is credited with saying to the ump, "Look, there are forty thousand people here who know that last pitch was a ball, tomato head!" Umpire Pinelli countered back, "Maybe so, but mine is the only opinion that counts."

One of the great catchers of all time, and a delight to quote, Yogi Berra, said in his book, *Ten Rings*, "When it comes to dealing with the home plate umpire, the big thing, don't turn around to bellyache, that's unforgivable. It's like saying to the fans, 'Hey look, this guy's blind as a bat.' Nobody likes being shown up like that."

"Eyes they have, but they see not," are the words of Jesus concerning the spiritual eyesight of the religious people of his day. Even in our "enlightened age" we are still of the same mind and heart, "blind as a bat."

We see the space shots on television but are blind to the poverty of our neighbor across town. We see the skin of the guy down the block but are blind to the need of his heart. We see the wonders of the universe but are blind to the Creator. Jesus is truthful, "They, seeing, see not."

In Weber's book, *As They See 'Em*, there is a call to worship by Reverend Dr. John C McCollister that is a hit.

"Almighty God, you who are called the great Umpire in this game of life, we are unsure of what uniform we should wear. While we may be Angels in spirit, in reality we are Giants in pride, Dodgers of responsibility and Tigers in ambition. When it comes to faith, we find ourselves in the minor leagues. When it comes to good works, we strike out. When it comes to knowledge of your Word, we are not even aware of the ground rules."

Open My Eyes, That I May See

Open my eyes, that I may see
Glimpses of truth Thou hast for me;
Place in my hands the wonderful key,
That shall unclasp and set me free.

Silently now I wait for Thee,
Ready, my God, Thy will to see;
Open my eyes, illumine me,
Spirit divine!
Clara Fiske Scott

CHAPTER 14

DON'T DIE ON THIRD

Heart

You've gotta have heart
All you really need is heart
When the odds are sayin' you'll never win,
That's when the grin should start.
Richard Adler and Jerry Ross

From Damn Yankees

A BALLPLAYER ACTUALLY DIED on third base during a baseball game, according to Mac Davis in his book, *Sports Shorts*. That astonishing occurrence took place around the turn of the twentieth century. Two outstanding semi-pro teams from Minnesota had won the attention of the baseball world. When these two teams met, one from Wilmar and one from Benson, fans came from hundreds of miles to witness the battle.

For nine innings, they played to a deadlock. Neither team was able to score the winning run. In the first half of the tenth, the Benson club scored a run. The Wilmar team then came to bat. With Theilman, the Wilmar pitcher, on first base, O'Toole smashed a terrific drive into the outfield. It looked like a sure home run, but Theilman, who was running in front of O'Toole, rounded third base and suddenly collapsed. O'Toole passed third base a few steps behind. Unable to pass him, O'Toole picked him up and carried him, throwing Theilman across home plate ahead of him and thus, winning the game. It was then determined that Theilman had died of a heart attack at third base!

It is sad but true, many people are dying on the third base of life. They seem to have everything the world can offer but yet cannot grasp the reality of life. They pause at third with a question mark instead of an exclamation point.

William J. Cameron, in his inspirational essay, *Don't Die on Third,* wrote, "Much as it is meant to have advanced that far, third base runs are not marked up on the scoreboard. Third base is not a destination -- it is the last way station on the road 'home.' The world is full of third bases." Cameron went on to remark, "Third base is opportunity, and opportunity is not arrival, it is only another point of departure ... the test of all you have is yet to come. No time for self applause on third, many a promising run has died there."

When Jesus Christ was here on earth, he met a man that seemed to have it all. He was young, rich and popular. He had everything going for him. If any man deserved to be a winner in life, it was this man. Yet, his life was incomplete and he knew it. So he came running to Jesus and asked, "Good Teacher, what must I do to inherit eternal life?" He knew that he was unsatisfied deep in his heart. The Bible tells us, Jesus loved this unusually gifted young man. He knew the man was sincere and wanted to do what was right and best. Speaking straight to his heart, Jesus said, "You lack one thing; go, sell what you have and give to the poor and come, follow me."

But the victorious words of the Savior were too much for him. The Bible records the tragic scene. "And he went away sorrowful; for he had great possessions." The rich young man, so close to victory, died spiritually at third base that day.

It is disappointing to lose a game, especially with a runner on third base. Leon "Red" Ames hurled a no-hit, no-run game on the opening day of the 1909 baseball season for thirteen innings. However, after the visiting team finally scored a run in the top of the fourteenth inning, he did not win the game. His New York Giants failed to score even though they had a runner at third, so the game was lost in the fourteenth inning 1 to 0.

The rally of a team that is behind and scores to win at virtually the last possible moment is probably the most exciting action in baseball. In

1951, when my twin and I were juniors in high school, we were glued to the radio listening to the play-by-play broadcast between the New York Giants and the Brooklyn Dodgers. We didn't realize we were about to hear one of the most famous ninth-inning rallies in baseball history.

The Giants had come back from 13½ games behind, at the end of the season, to catch the leading Dodgers and force a three game playoff. The teams split the first two games. In the third game, at the bottom of the ninth inning, the Dodgers were ahead 4-2. Then, the Giants got ground singles by Alvin Dark and Don Mueller. That put two runners on base with one out. This brought up, Bobby Thompson, who then lined the second pitch into the left field stands for a three-run homer! It gave the Giants a 5-4 victory and the pennant! As Dodger rooters, Fred and I were stunned to hear Russ Hodges, the radio broadcaster screaming, "The Giants win the pennant; the Giants win the pennant!" This home run was dubbed, "the shot heard around the world!" We joined the ranks of Dodger fans … "Wait 'til next year!"

Baseball becomes especially exciting when a runner is on third base. It's a time when every fan is sitting on the edge of his seat. The slightest bobble of the ball or missed throw may give the runner a chance to break for home with the score.

Probably, the most dangerous runner at third base, was Jackie Robinson of the Brooklyn Dodgers. His daring base thefts on the diamond made him one of the most feared base runners. Jackie, knew the game; he knew catchers movements and pitchers particular ways of throwing toward the plate. He had an innate instinct to measure the speed of a five-ounce ball delivered at ninety miles and hour, against the time it took him to hurl his body down the ninety- foot base line to the plate.

My first year as a pro was Robinson's next-to-last year as an active player. Jackie's career was almost behind him then and what a brilliant performer he was! In 1947, as the first black to play in major league baseball, he was voted "Rookie of the Year." Two years later, he was voted the National League's "Most Valuable Player" and that year he also won the batting championship. After leading the Dodgers into the World Series three times and regularly being a National League All Star, Jackie was enshrined in the Hall of Fame in 1962.

I saw Jackie in action in March of 1955, the year he led the Dodgers to their first World Series championship. Spring training was in full swing and on that lazy, sunny afternoon, the St. Louis Cardinals came to Vero Beach to play an exhibition game against our Dodgers. Jackie was in the starting lineup, playing at third base. Below his ball cap you could see the gray hair of his side burns, causing him to look more like a distinguished doctor or lawyer than a ball player. He still commanded the respect of every player on both teams as he stepped onto the field. Without a doubt, he was the elder statesman and the club leader.

The score was tied in the bottom half of the ninth inning. Jackie hit a stand- up triple off the great Cardinal reliever, Lindy McDaniel, who was a former University of Oklahoma teammate of mine. That afternoon, Robinson displayed his famous daring base running, which made him so feared by opposing teams. Back and forth on the third base line he ran with quick starts and stops. Sometimes he came to a complete standstill, as if taunting Lindy to throw him out.

For Jackie to steal home in a Spring Training Grape fruit League game was unheard of. He had no reason to risk himself of potential injury in a nothing game. But that was who he was: Jackie's heart beat wouldn't let him to ever, "Die on Third!"

The cool, calm McDaniel seemed to completely ignore Robinson's antics and concentrated on his pitches to the batter, Don Demeter. Lindy was a right hand, side arm pitcher, which enabled him to stare at Robinson, as he pitched. However, Jackie continued his intimidation, with stops and starts back and forth along the base path.

Suddenly, Jackie made his famous explosive lunge toward home plate. In the next instant, McDaniel, hurriedly threw to the plate, but his quick side arm throw could not catch the speeding Robinson. Jackie slid with his foot outthrust across home plate ahead of the throw to score the winning run!

It was one of the most breathtaking plays I have ever seen! That steal home by Jackie, was just the warm up of what he was to mean to the Dodgers that year. Even with a nagging injury to his leg, he was the spark that took the slumping Dodgers into the World Series, to become World Champions in 1955. As George Vecsy said in his historical book, *Baseball*, "It was a biblical New Year that finally arrived and church bells tolled all over Brooklyn."

Jackie's slogan in baseball was, "Don't die on third!" That same strong heartbeat made him a hero on and off the field. He cut across the cultural barriers and helped race relations for all Americans.

During my pastorates, I was warmly received in the black communities, especially when they found I was a former Dodger. The Dodgers opened the door for them to have an equal footing through all avenues of life and they appreciated it. In fact, to this day as a minister of the Gospel, my Dodger background has been a blessing. Some people get the idea that a pastor is so heavenly minded that he is of no earthly good. But the knowledge that I once pitched in the minors for the Dodgers, has helped people identify me as a real person.

Third base is so close, only ninety feet away, yet so far from home plate. No game was ever won at third base; it takes home plate to get the win. There is a term in baseball; "Run it out." This is what a player should do every time he is on base or after he hits the ball. Although, it looks like the ball will be caught in the outfield or played in the infield, he should still run as hard as he can. The defensive player may make an error in fielding or throwing the ball, so run it out!

When Derek Jeter received the 2009 Sportsman of the Year Award, Tom Verducci of *Sports Illustrated,* tells the terrific insight given by Jeter's manager about this Yankee shortstop. "Here you have one of the best players in the game, who already had made his money and had his four championships by then, and he's down there and runs in the seventh inning, running like that. It was a way of showing our guys, 'You think you're running hard, until you see a champion and a Hall of Famer run.' It wasn't that our guys were dogging it, but this is different. If Derek Jeter can run all out all the time, everybody else better personally ask themselves why they can't."

The apostle Paul wrote, "I have fought the good fight, I have finished the race, I have kept the faith!"

My twin brother and me in our rookie year in the Minors with the Dodgers.

My twin brother, Fred, wrote this poem during his third year of pro baseball in 1957. He was playing center field for the Baltimore Orioles, Paris, Texas, baseball club.

On the Third Base of Life Without a Score

The bat was swung
tThe ball was met
He ran toward first
He had a hit.

Eagerly he eyed That second base;
With a burst of speed,
Slid on his face.

"Safe!" yelled the ump.
The roar of the crowd
Made the player feel good,
And mighty proud.

Ready and tense
He must get to third.
The coach gave a sign
He had given the word.

Dust and dirt and An impact of cleats –
He was fightin' for third.
There were no retreats.

"Safe!" yelled the ump
To the amazement of all,
For the man guarding third
Had dropped the ball!

Third base was conquered
And it was for real.
What a great accomplishment
And such a great thrill!

> But the player forgot
> About the base ahead.
> "Third base doesn't count"
> The score keeper said
>
> So, when you're at bat
> And you get a hit,
> Remember on third
> You've not scored yet.
>
> Home by God's grace
> With Christ evermore
> But not on third base
> Without faith's score.

In the Bible, Jesus tells a story of a last minute revival for a dying young man. This guy was standing on the third base of life and needed a rally to surge him on at the last possible moment. Calamity was about to take over, because his pattern of life was one of rebellion. He wanted to eat, drink and be merry so much, he was willing to risk his life to "die on third." Even though loved at home, he wanted his own kind of life, right or wrong, and he wanted it now!

So, arrogantly and selfishly, he demanded his share of the inheritance before it was his time to receive it. His father was gracious and let him have it, anyway. As soon as he could get his stuff together, he moved a long distance from home. He was determined that he was not going live a "nobody," monotonous life. He was going to have fun, at any cost.

He lived it up, and did he ever! He was footloose and fancy free. The Bible underscores it as "riotous living." He wanted the good times to roll and keep on rolling. It wasn't long before he squandered all of his wealth and then a severe famine hit the land, causing him to be at the point of starvation. He tried to find a job anywhere he could. Work for party boys was scarce. At last, he found one and of all jobs, it was on a pig farm, slopping the hogs, which was terribly degrading for a Jewish boy. But he was so broke and hungry he even wanted to eat the food he fed the pigs!

Jesus said, "It was then that he came to himself, 'How many hired servants are in my father's house and they have food to spare. Here I am and I'm starving to death. I'm going home and confess to my father that I have sinned against him and heaven. I'll tell him that I am no more worthy to be called a son, but let me be a hired servant instead'."

Jesus continued, "When the boy's father saw him coming down the long road to the house, "he ran to meet him and filled with loving pity scooped him up and gave him a big bear hug!" A royal welcome was his; the best robe was given to him, the ring of the family was placed on his finger and a feast with music was given in his honor. He was not deserving of all this; he should have "died on third," but he came home and found forgiveness and a new life. With compassionate words, the father concluded, "He was dead and is alive again; he was lost and is found."

Ring the bells of Heaven!
There is joy today,
For a soul, returning from the wild!
See the Father meets him
Out upon the way,
Welcoming His weary
Wandering child.
William O. Cushing

Baseball was designed around home. The diamond's layout always begins and ends at home plate. The greatest hit is the home run. Players hit, bunt, run, walk and slide to get home to win the game. We sing at the home-half of the seventh inning, "Let's root, root, root for the home team."

Jesus was raised in a home in Nazareth; however, it's ironic and almost sad that Jesus did not have a home of his own. Jesus said, "Foxes have holes and birds of the air have nests, but the Son of Man has no place to lay his head." Jesus enjoyed home life. He performed his first miracle at a home wedding in Nazareth. On his way to the Cross he stopped and stayed a while in Bethany at the home of his friends, Lazarus, Mary and Martha. He promised us a home, "In my Father's house are many dwelling places … I am going away to prepare a place for you. . . I will come back and receive you to myself, so where I am, you may be also."

Final Score

Eventually there's a final score
when games have ended
when they're over –- no more.
Lee Bennett Hopkins

I was an eleven year old boy when I first started playing baseball by throwing catch with my twin brother, Fred. That same year we trusted Jesus as our Savior and became Christians. One of the first hymns I learned was a simple little melody with these words:

Softly and tenderly Jesus is calling,
Calling for you and for me;
See, on the portals He's waiting and watching,
Watching for you and for me.
Come home, come home;
You who are weary, come home.
Earnestly, tenderly, Jesus is calling,
Calling, O sinner, come home!
William Thompson

Facing Death in the Lake's Edge

by Frank Minton

It was a warm Saturday morning November 20, 2021, when I decided to water flowers that were planted a few days prior. There was no thought on that bright sunny day, I was about to face death!

Our townhouse in Walden on Lake Conroe, Montgomery, Texas is only ten feet or so from the water's edge. As a retired Baptist minister, my wife Joyce and I have felt blessed to have lived seventeen years in a place with such beautiful surroundings: a 180° view of the marina with dozens of docked sailboats, further away in clear sight the yacht club's stately building and across the water several large three storied condos.

I was walking backward pulling on a water hose not realizing how near I was to the lake's edge. As I tugged at the hose, suddenly I plunged backward, headfirst into the cold lake waters, clothes, shoes and all!

How long I was under the water, I can only imagine. In the splash, I lost my glasses and partial dentures. In fact, the dentures got caught up in my open mouth and with the water pouring in I managed to grab it and did my best to throw it toward the bulkhead area.

When I surfaced, regaining my feet, I heard a lady's voice coming from the condo area. I did not realize this was the voice of a "guardian angel."

"Are you all right?" she hollered. I immediately yelled back, "Sure, I'm OK!" as I waved but I wasn't OK. I did not know it was impossible for me to get out of the lake in my own strength. I was trapped!

The water was up to my chest and the bulkhead wall

was over a foot higher with nothing for me to grab. My fingers could not penetrate the wood top.

I knew how to swim and swam in that same area when we first moved to our home. This was before the final bulkheads were built walling off the easy path in and out of the lake. Trying to swim to a more acceptable place in full clothing was not an option. It was more than 200 yards to the condo area and the sailboat docks were higher than the bulkhead wall.

My younger prowess as a Brooklyn Dodger / Los Angeles baseball player was gone. Even my continued workouts that gave me an athletic look were no match to what I was up against. Frantically, I bashed my knees against the concrete walls to help lift up my body but to no avail. I knew then I didn't have a chance to get out by myself.

My continued calling to Joyce was so weak I just stopped trying. No way Joyce could hear me!

I began moving step by step toward our patio area where our wall-to-wall large windows were located. Perhaps, I thought, Joyce might be able to clearly see me.

Suddenly, without warning, I found myself seeing a group of happy people going to a party. The men were well dressed in slack pants and the women were wearing high-heeled shoes and attractive dresses. I thought, "I'll join them but what's all this water doing at a party?" That's when I regained my consciousness and stood up to get back to reality.

I continued to move more slowly toward my goal. Out ahead I could see our boat dock, which is connected to the bulkhead boards. It now seemed even more difficult to move forward.

Just as I was in full view of the windows, I experienced the same happy partygoers. This time I was more determined to join them. Again, the rushing water invaded the party group. Up I came! This time with the fear of drowning. I felt that another episode would be my last. I was facing death!

As I continued to inch forward, I slowly reached the corner of the bulk board and our boat dock. At this moment, I felt totally exhausted and could barely stand up so I clung even closer to the bulk board.

I was still in chest-high cold water and hoped if I could hang on long enough, Joyce could see me. I felt huge anxiety because I knew I was stuck! Energy and time were running out.

As I hung on, I looked up and to my grateful surprise, a lady was standing in front of me. Weakly I begged, "That's my house, go get my wife!" I assumed she was the lady from the condos across the lake.

She immediately left and in a quick minute, Joyce was at the lakeside back door.

"Honey, get the stepladder in the utility room!" I weakly called out to her.

As Joyce retrieved the ladder, the unknown lady grabbed it out of her hands and rushed to me. She quickly lowered the ladder into the water to me.

I hardly had enough strength to take step one, then two and as the ladder was sinking in the mud, I wobbly made one big step on the white handle of the ladder. With a push from my foot, I crawled onto the deck on my stomach and laid there so exhausted I couldn't move.

When I looked up, there were six blue-uniformed 911 men. Two guys picked me up and dragged me to our patio where Joyce was waiting. As I sat dazed on the patio edge I said, "Just let me rest here a while, then I'll go into the house to lay down."

"You're not going anywhere," came a terse remark. "What hospital do you want us to take you?" With that, they lifted me onto a gurney. As they put me into the waiting ambulance, I saw a fire truck and two police squad cars. The force was present!

My "guardian Angel" had disappeared after the 911 men appeared. Who was she? My wife only caught her name "Debbie." She may live across the lake in one of the three-storied condos -perhaps? Yet no further contact.

Without a doubt, God allowed this "guardian Angel" to see me fall into the lake and led her to follow through to my rescue, in person and by calling 911. She was God's messenger for me. It was a "God thing!"

I spent a week in Hospital care with a heart catheterization by my cardiologist Dr. Earl Mangin which revealed no heart attack. My knees were so battered and bruised from trying to get out that it took three days before I could walk.

Our family physician, Dr. Matthew Simpson exclaimed, "According to the hospital report, your strength was almost gone." Then he added, "If you had not been rescued soon you probably would have drowned."

Today reflecting upon my near-death experience causes me to feel closer to God. Certainly, God has yet a plan for my life. Perhaps only in a small way but that's good enough! I continue to thank Him for His "Guardian Angel!"

We found her! Debbie is a librarian. Yes, she lives in one of the three-storied condos across the lake. She said, "I was on the phone when I saw a big splash and then saw you. I know the lake, knew you were in trouble and couldn't get out. So I rushed out and drove my car to your place and while driving called 911." God bless her!

I claim God's promise in Psalms 91:11, "For He will command His angels concerning you to guard you in all your ways." God kept His Word!

The Courier | yourconroenews.com

Tuesday, March 8, 2022 | A3

Earl Schneider was one of at least six fatalities on the waters of Lake Conroe in 2021, which public safety officials said was one of the deadliest of recent years at the popular destination.

Additionally, in August, an 80year-old man died at a hospital after a double-decker tour boat he was a passenger on wrecked on the lake.

I am grateful of was not number?!

Frank D Minton